THE ULTIMATE STOCK MARKET INVESTING
FOR BEGINNERS GUIDE

The Millennial's Roadmap To Wealth;
Stock Investing In The Digital Age

MEGAN REED

© Copyright 2024 - All rights reserved.

The content of this book may not be reproduced, duplicated, or transmitted without the direct written permission of the author or publisher.

Under no circumstances shall the publisher or author be held legally responsible or liable for any damage, repair, or monetary loss due to the information contained within this book, whether direct or indirect. You are responsible for your own choices, actions, and outcomes.

Legal Notice:

This book is protected by copyright. This book is for personal use only. You may not modify, distribute, sell, use, quote, or paraphrase any part of or the content within this book without the author's consent.

Disclaimer Notice:

Please be aware that the information contained within this document is for educational and entertainment purposes only. Every effort has been made to present accurate, up-to-date, reliable, and complete information. No warranties of any kind are declared or implied. Readers acknowledge that the author is not providing legal, financial, medical, or professional advice. The content of this book has been derived from various sources. Consult a licensed professional before attempting any techniques described in this book.

By reading this document, the reader agrees that under no circumstances is the author responsible for any loss, direct or indirect, incurred as a result of using the information contained in this document, including, but not limited to — errors, omissions, or inaccuracies.

Contents

Introduction	1
1. Laying the Foundation	3
2. Getting Started with Investing	13
3. Risk Management and Diversification	26
4. Analyzing Stocks and Making Decisions	37
5. Long-Term Investment Strategies	49
6. Avoiding Common Pitfalls	61
7. Continuous Learning and Improvement	71
8. Building Financial Resilience	81
9. Empowerment and Independence	92
Conclusion	104
About The Author	106
Also By Megan Reed	107
References	109

Introduction

"The biggest risk is not taking any risk... In a world that's changing really quickly, the only strategy that is guaranteed to fail is not taking risks."

— Mark Zuckerberg

When I was in my early twenties, I was living paycheck to paycheck, anxious about the future. I had just moved to a new city and was struggling to make ends meet. One day, I decided to take a bold step. I invested a small amount of money in the stock market. It wasn't much, but it was a start. That small step changed my life. Over time, I learned more, made smarter choices, and watched my investments grow. Today, I want to share that journey with you.

The purpose of this book is to demystify stock market investing for beginners. It's designed to provide you with a step-by-step approach, starting with the basics and gradually moving to more advanced strategies. Whether you're new to investing or just looking to refine your approach, this book aims to equip you with the knowledge and confidence to make informed investment choices.

What sets this book apart is its holistic view of investing. Unlike many guides that promise quick wins or follow trendy advice, this book emphasizes a gradual, steady approach. You'll learn how to start small, understand risk management, and build a diversified portfolio tailored to your goals and risk tolerance.

Why focus on Millennials and Gen Z? Because you face unique financial challenges and opportunities. You are tech-savvy, socially conscious, and looking for ways to secure your financial future. The digital age presents new tools and platforms for investing, but it also comes with its own set of risks. This book addresses those challenges and provides practical solutions.

The structure of the book is designed to be both comprehensive and easy to follow. We start with the fundamentals of the stock market, explaining key concepts and terminology. Then we move into practical strategies, covering topics like stock selection, portfolio diversification, and risk management. Each chapter builds on the previous one, ensuring a smooth learning curve.

Financial education is more important than ever. In today's fast-paced world, understanding how to manage your money and invest wisely can make a significant difference in your quality of life. This book aims to empower you with the knowledge and tools you need to take control of your financial future.

My personal vision and mission are to make investing accessible to everyone. I have been investing for over 20 years and have seen firsthand the transformative power of smart investing. I want to share my insights and experiences to help you avoid common pitfalls and achieve financial independence.

So, are you ready to take control of your financial future? This book will guide you through the process, providing actionable steps and practical advice. By the end, you'll have a clear roadmap for starting your investment journey and building wealth over time.

In the upcoming chapters, we'll dive into the specifics of stock market investing. You'll learn how to analyze stocks, build a diversified portfolio, and manage risk. We'll also explore the latest tools and platforms that can help you invest more effectively in the digital age.

Let's get started on this exciting journey together. Your future self will thank you for the steps you take today.

Chapter 1
Laying the Foundation

"I think you have to learn that there's a company behind every stock and that there's only one reason why stocks go up. Companies go from doing poorly to doing well, or small companies grow to large companies."

Peter Lynch

When I first dipped my toes into the world of investing, I was overwhelmed. Stock market jargon flew over my head, and the sheer volume of information seemed insurmountable. One evening, I sat at my kitchen table, staring at a list of stock names and feeling utterly lost. I decided to pick one stock—just one—based on a recommendation from a friend. That simple act of buying my first share was the beginning of a significant shift in my financial life. It wasn't just about the potential for financial gain; it was about taking control, learning, and growing. This chapter aims to provide you with the foundational knowledge you need to make that first step without feeling overwhelmed.

1.1 Understanding Stocks: The Building Blocks of Wealth

Stocks are more than just numbers on a screen; they are a slice of a company's ownership. When you buy a stock, you're purchasing a small piece of that company, known as a share. This share represents a claim on part of the company's assets and earnings. Over time, as the company grows and becomes more profitable, the value of your shares can increase, leading to capital gains. This potential for growth is what makes stocks a powerful tool for wealth-building. By investing in stocks, you're not just betting on a company's success but also your financial future.

There are two main types of stocks: common stocks and preferred stocks. Common stocks are what most people think of when they hear the term "stocks." They typically give shareholders voting rights, allowing them to have a say in certain company decisions. However, common stocks can be more volatile, meaning their prices can fluctuate widely. Preferred stocks, on the other hand, offer fixed dividends and have priority over common stocks when it comes to dividend payments and asset liquidation. They don't usually come with voting rights, but they are generally less volatile and provide a steadier income stream. Understanding the differences between these types of stocks can help you make more informed investment decisions.

Dividends are another crucial aspect of stock investing. They are payments made by a corporation to its shareholders, usually as a distribution of profits. Not all companies pay dividends, but those that do often provide a steady income stream, which can be particularly appealing if you're looking for regular income from your investments. Dividend-paying stocks can be an excellent addition to your portfolio, offering both potential capital gains and income. For example, companies like PepsiCo and Johnson & Johnson are known for their reliable dividend payments, making them attractive to many investors.

Stock exchanges play a vital role in the stock market ecosystem. They function as marketplaces where stocks are bought and sold. The New York Stock Exchange (NYSE) and Nasdaq are two of the most well-known stock exchanges in the United States. Each operates differently but serves the same essential purpose: facilitating the trading of stocks. The NYSE, often considered more prestigious, operates as an auction market with designated market makers, while the Nasdaq functions as a dealer market with multiple market makers. Trades on the NYSE are made directly between participants, while Nasdaq trades are executed through dealers. Both exchanges help determine the market prices of stocks, providing a platform for liquidity and price discovery.

Understanding these foundational concepts is critical as you begin your investment journey. Stocks offer a gateway to building wealth, but they come with their complexities. Knowing what stocks are, the types available, the role of dividends, and the function of stock exchanges will give you a solid starting point. You'll be better equipped to navigate the stock market and make informed decisions that align with your financial goals. As we proceed, we'll delve deeper into these topics, providing you with the tools and knowledge to become a confident and successful investor.

1.2 The Mechanics of the Stock Market: How It Really Works

Understanding how stock prices are determined is crucial for any aspiring investor. At its core, stock price is influenced by supply and demand. When demand for a stock increases—perhaps due to positive news about the company or strong earnings reports—the price typically rises. Conversely, if demand decreases, the price falls. For instance, if a company like Apple announces a groundbreaking new product, more people might want to buy its stock, driving the price up. On the other hand, if a company faces a scandal or disappointing earnings, the value may plummet as investors rush to sell.

Beyond supply and demand, several other factors play a role in determining stock prices. Company performance is a significant influence. When a company reports strong earnings or shows potential for future growth, its stock price may rise. Market sentiment also plays a crucial role. If investors believe that a company will perform well in the future, they are more likely to buy its stock, driving up the price. Conversely, if pessimism surrounds the company's prospects, the stock price may fall. Economic indicators, such as interest rates and inflation, can also impact stock prices. For example, lower interest rates often make borrowing cheaper, which can spur economic growth and boost stock prices.

The stock market is a bustling ecosystem filled with various participants, each playing a distinct role. Retail investors are individuals like you and me, buying and selling stocks through personal brokerage accounts. These investors might be someone saving for retirement or a young professional looking to grow their wealth. Institutional investors, such as mutual funds, pension funds, and insurance companies, operate on a much larger scale. They manage vast sums of money and can significantly influence stock prices through their trading activities. Then, there are market makers, who ensure liquidity in the market by being ready to buy or sell stocks at any given time. These entities help maintain the balance between buyers and sellers, ensuring that trades can be executed smoothly.

Market indices are essential tools for gauging overall market performance. The S&P 500, for example, tracks the performance of 500 large-cap companies in the U.S. It serves as a barometer for the overall health of the stock market and is often used as a benchmark for investment performance. The Dow Jones Industrial Average, consisting of 30 significant companies, is one of the oldest and most well-known indices. It provides a snapshot of market trends and economic health. The Nasdaq Composite, known for its tech-heavy composition, includes over 3,000 stocks and is a key indicator of the technology sector's performance. These indices help investors understand market trends and make informed decisions about their portfolios.

Regulation is the backbone of market integrity and investor protection. The Securities and Exchange Commission (SEC) plays a pivotal role in enforcing laws against market manipulation and fraud. For example, the SEC requires companies to disclose important financial information, ensuring transparency and helping investors make informed decisions. Regulations also ensure fairness, preventing practices that could disadvantage individual investors. This regulatory framework is vital for maintaining trust in the stock market, allowing it to function efficiently and fairly. Without such oversight, the market would be prone to abuses and manipulation, eroding investor confidence.

Imagine a bustling marketplace where vendors shout out prices, buyers haggle, and deals are struck constantly. This vibrant scene is akin to the stock exchange. It's where stocks are bought and sold, prices are negotiated, and trades are executed. The NYSE, with its iconic trading floor, and Nasdaq, operating entirely electronically, are the epicenters of this activity. Each has its unique methods and characteristics, catering to different types of companies and investors. The NYSE, often seen as more prestigious, lists many established companies. At the same time, the Nasdaq is known for its innovative and growth-oriented firms. Whether you're buying shares of a tech giant on the Nasdaq or an industry stalwart on the NYSE, these exchanges facilitate the transactions that drive the stock market.

In this chapter, we've laid down the foundational elements that influence the stock market. From the forces of supply and demand to the critical role of market participants and indices, understanding these mechanics will empower you to navigate the stock market with greater confidence.

1.3 Setting Up Your First Brokerage Account: A Step-by-Step Guide

Choosing the right brokerage can feel like a daunting task, but it's a crucial step in your investment path. The brokerage you select will be your gateway to the stock market, so it's important to consider several key factors. Look for brokerages that offer low or no commission fees to keep your costs minimal. This is especially important if you're just starting out and don't have a lot of capital to invest. For instance, many online brokerages now offer commission-free trading, making it easier and cheaper to buy and sell stocks. The usability of the platform is another critical factor. You'll want a user-friendly interface that makes it easy to execute trades, check your portfolio, and access educational resources. Some platforms come with additional tools like research reports, stock screeners, and educational content, which can be incredibly helpful for beginners. Think of it like choosing a smartphone—you want something intuitive and loaded with features that make your life easier.

The next step is setting up your account. This process is straightforward but requires attention to detail. Begin by filling out an application with your personal information. You'll need identification documents like a driver's license or passport. This step ensures that your account is secure and complies with regulatory requirements. Once your application is approved, you'll need to fund your account. Most brokerages allow you to link your bank account for easy fund transfers. This setup makes it simple to move money into your brokerage account whenever you're ready to invest. Some brokerages also offer other funding options like wire transfers or checks, but linking your bank account is typically the most convenient method.

Understanding the types of brokerage accounts available is essential for aligning your investment strategy with your financial goals. There are primarily two types of accounts: cash accounts and margin accounts. A cash account is straightforward—you can only buy securities with the money you have in your account. This type of account is ideal for beginners as it limits risk and encourages disciplined investing. On the other hand, a margin account allows you to borrow funds to trade, using your investments as collateral. While margin trading can amplify your gains, it also increases your risk. If the market moves against you, you could face significant losses and even owe more than you initially invested. It's crucial to understand these risks before deciding on a margin account.

Brokerage features can significantly enhance your investing experience, especially if you're new to the stock market. Research tools and educational resources are invaluable. Some brokerages offer in-depth market analysis, stock screeners, and financial news updates, helping you make informed decisions. These tools can be particularly useful when you're evaluating potential investments and need reliable data to back up your choices. Another essential feature is robust customer support. As a beginner, you'll likely have questions or encounter issues that need resolution. Brokerages with strong customer support can provide timely and helpful assistance, ensuring that your investing experience is smooth and stress-free. Whether it's a live chat feature, a comprehensive FAQ section, or dedicated customer service lines, having access to support can make a significant difference.

When setting up your first brokerage account, think of it as laying the foundation for your investment activities. The choices you make here will have long-term implications, so take the time to research and select the best options for your needs. Evaluate the fees, usability, and additional resources offered by different brokerages. Consider starting with a cash account to keep risks manageable, and make sure the platform provides the tools and support you need to succeed. This initial setup is more than just a formality; it's a strategic move that sets the stage for your future financial growth.

1.4 Decoding Financial Jargon: Your Investment Glossary

Navigating the stock market often feels like learning a new language. The jargon can be intimidating, but understanding key terms is crucial for making informed decisions. Let's start with market capitalization. Market capitalization, or market cap, refers to the total market value of a company's outstanding shares. Think of it as the price tag for the entire company. For example, if a company has one million shares outstanding and each share is priced at $50, the market cap is $50 million. Knowing the market cap helps you understand the size and stability of a company. Small-cap stocks, for instance, generally have a market cap of less than $2 billion and can offer high growth potential but come with higher risk. On the other hand, large-cap stocks, with a market cap exceeding $10 billion, are usually more stable but offer slower growth.

The Price-to-Earnings ratio, or P/E ratio, is another fundamental term. The P/E ratio compares a company's current share price to its earnings per share (EPS). Think of it like a price tag at a store showing how much you're paying for each dollar of earnings. For example, if a company's share price is $30 and its EPS is $2, the P/E ratio is 15. This means investors are willing to pay $15 for every $1 of earnings. A high P/E ratio might indicate that a stock is overvalued, suggesting investors expect high growth in the future. Conversely, a low P/E ratio could suggest that the stock is undervalued or that the company's future growth prospects are not promising. Understanding the P/E ratio helps you gauge a company's valuation and make more informed investment choices.

Next, let's talk about dividends. Dividends are payments made by a corporation to its shareholders, usually as a distribution of profits. Not all companies pay dividends, but those that do often provide a steady income stream, which can be particularly appealing if you're looking for regular income from your investments. Dividend yield is a related term that helps you understand the return on investment from dividends alone. It's calculated by dividing the annual dividend payment by the stock's current price. For example, if a stock priced at $100 pays an annual dividend of $4, the dividend yield is 4%. This metric is vital for income-focused investors who rely on their investments to generate cash flow.

Another critical term is the beta coefficient, often just called beta. Beta measures a stock's volatility in relation to the overall market. A beta of 1 indicates that the stock's price moves with the market. A beta greater than 1 means the stock is more volatile than the market, while a beta less than 1 means it's less volatile. For instance, a stock with a beta of 1.5 is expected to be 50% more volatile than the market. Understanding beta helps you assess the risk associated with a particular stock and how it might behave in different market conditions.

Now, let's discuss earnings per share (EPS). EPS is a company's profit divided by the number of outstanding shares of its common stock. It's a key indicator of a company's profitability. For example, if a company earns $10 million in profit and has 5 million shares outstanding, its EPS is $2. Investors use EPS to gauge a company's performance and profitability. Higher EPS often indicates a more profitable company, but it's essential to compare EPS with other companies in the same industry to get a meaningful perspective.

Another term you'll encounter is the dividend payout ratio. This ratio measures the percentage of earnings distributed to shareholders in the form of dividends. It's calculated by dividing the annual dividends per share by the EPS. For instance, if a company has an EPS of $5 and pays an annual dividend of $2, the payout ratio is 40%. A lower payout ratio might suggest that the company is reinvesting more of its earnings into growth, while a higher ratio could indicate a more mature company returning profits to shareholders.

Understanding these terms is crucial for making informed investment decisions. They provide insights into a company's financial health, valuation, and potential risks. As you become more familiar with this jargon, you'll find it easier to analyze stocks and build a robust investment portfolio. This knowledge will empower you to navigate the stock market with confidence, making choices that align with your financial goals.

1.5 The Importance of Financial Education: Bridging the Knowledge Gap

Many young adults find themselves thrust into the world of personal finance with little to no formal education on the subject. Schools often do not offer comprehensive financial literacy programs, leaving students unprepared for real-world financial decisions. Imagine graduating from college with a degree but lacking the skills to manage a budget, understand credit, or make informed investment choices. This lack of financial education has significant consequences. Without a solid grasp of basic financial concepts, you might find yourself making poor financial decisions, falling into debt, or missing out on opportunities to build wealth through investments. The gap in financial education leaves many feeling overwhelmed and anxious about their financial future, unsure of where to start or whom to trust for advice.

Financial literacy, on the other hand, is empowering. It equips you with the knowledge and skills needed to make sound financial decisions, avoid common pitfalls, and achieve financial independence. Understanding financial concepts can help you avoid scams and emotional decision-making, which are common traps for inexperienced investors. For instance, knowing how to read a financial statement or analyze a company's performance can prevent you from investing in a failing business. Educated investors are more likely to build diversified portfolios, plan for long-term goals, and adapt to changing market conditions. This knowledge fosters confidence and a sense of control over your financial destiny, enabling you to navigate the complexities of the stock market with greater ease.

To bridge this knowledge gap, numerous resources are available to help you deepen your financial understanding. Books like "Rich Dad, Poor Dad" by Robert Kiyosaki and "The Intelligent Investor" by Benjamin Graham offer valuable insights into personal finance and investing. These books break down complex concepts into relatable, actionable advice, making them excellent starting points for anyone looking to improve their financial literacy. Websites like Investopedia and Khan Academy provide free educational resources on a wide range of financial topics, from basic budgeting to advanced investment strategies. These platforms offer articles, videos, and interactive tutorials that cater to different learning styles, making it easier for you to grasp difficult concepts.

Taking a proactive approach to financial education is crucial. Don't wait for knowledge to come to you; seek it out. Join online forums and communities, such as Reddit's r/PersonalFinance, where you can learn from others and share experiences. These communities are filled with people who have been in your shoes and can offer practical advice and support. Attend webinars and workshops hosted by financial experts to stay updated on the latest trends and strategies. Many of these events are free and provide opportunities to ask questions and interact with professionals who can guide you. The more you engage with these resources, the more confident and knowledgeable you will become.

Financial education is not a one-time event but an ongoing process. The financial world is dynamic, with new tools, strategies, and regulations emerging regularly. Staying informed and continuously learning is key to maintaining and growing your financial health. Set aside time each week to read financial news, study investment strategies, and review your financial plan. This habit will keep you up-to-date and help you make informed decisions. By investing in your financial education, you are investing in your future, laying the groundwork for a secure and prosperous life.

The journey to financial literacy is a rewarding one. It starts with small steps—reading a book, joining a forum, attending a webinar—but these steps accumulate, leading to significant improvements in your financial well-being. As you continue to learn and grow, you'll find yourself more confident in making investment decisions, more adept at managing your money, and more prepared to achieve your financial goals. The knowledge you gain will not only benefit you but can also be shared with friends and family, creating a ripple effect that promotes financial literacy within your community.

In the next chapter, we will explore practical strategies for getting started with investing, providing you with actionable steps and insights to help you begin your investment journey with confidence.

Chapter 2
Getting Started with Investing

"The rich invest in time, the poor invest in money."
Warren Buffett

I remember the thrill of holding my first paycheck. It wasn't just a piece of paper; it was a symbol of my independence and hard work. But as quickly as the excitement came, so did the realization of my financial responsibilities. How could I make this money work for me? How could I ensure that I wouldn't always be living from one paycheck to the next? That's when I decided to start investing. It was a modest beginning, with only $100, but it was a crucial step that set the foundation for my financial future.

2.1 Investing with $100: Your First Steps

Starting small is not just a practical approach; it's a smart strategy. Investing with $100 allows you to dip your toes into the stock market without risking significant capital. This modest amount is enough to get you started, build your confidence, and gain valuable experience. Think of it as a learning fee—one that could pay off significantly in the long run. When you start with a small amount, the stakes are lower, making it easier to recover from any mistakes and learn from them. This approach also helps you get accustomed to the mechanics of investing, such as placing orders and tracking your portfolio.

Low-cost investment options are ideal for beginners with limited funds. One such option is fractional shares, which allow you to buy a portion of a stock rather than a whole share. This means you can invest in high-priced stocks like Amazon or Tesla without needing thousands of dollars. Fractional shares democratize investing, making it accessible to everyone, regardless of their budget. Another excellent option is Exchange-Traded Funds (ETFs). These funds pool money from many investors to buy a diversified portfolio of stocks, bonds, or other assets. ETFs offer diversification at a low cost, reducing the risk associated with investing in individual stocks. They are an excellent way to spread your investment across multiple assets, lowering your overall risk.

To invest your first $100 effectively, follow these steps:

- First, choose a brokerage that offers no minimum deposit requirements. Many platforms, like Robinhood and Fidelity, allow you to start with as little as $1. Once you've selected your brokerage, open an account and fund it with your $100.

- Next, decide between buying fractional shares or an ETF. If you choose fractional shares, research high-quality stocks that interest you and allocate your funds accordingly. If you opt for an ETF, look for one with low fees and broad market exposure. For example, the Vanguard Total Stock Market ETF (VTI) offers exposure to the entire U.S. stock market with a low expense ratio.

- Finally, place your order and monitor your investment. Keep an eye on market trends and consider setting up alerts to stay informed about significant changes.

Starting early has profound benefits, thanks to the power of compounding. Compounding is the process where the returns on your investment generate their returns, leading to exponential growth over time. Even a small initial investment can grow substantially with consistent contributions and time. For example, if you invest $100 at an annual return of 7% and add $100 each month, your investment could grow to over $40,000 in 20 years. The key is consistency and patience. By starting early, you give your money more time to grow, taking full advantage of compounding. This approach can significantly enhance your financial future, providing you with more resources and opportunities down the line.

To illustrate the impact of starting small and early, let's consider a simple exercise. Imagine you invest $100 today and continue to invest $100 each month. Over the years, as you gain experience and confidence, you can gradually increase your contributions. Use the table below to track your progress and visualize the growth of your investments over time.

Investment Growth Tracker

This tracker helps you see the long-term benefits of starting small and investing consistently. It also serves as a motivational tool, showing you the potential growth of your investments. By taking these initial steps and maintaining a disciplined approach, you can set yourself on a path to financial success.

2.2 Selecting Your First Stocks: Criteria for Beginners

Before you dive into selecting your first stocks, it's crucial to understand the importance of research. Thorough research is the backbone of informed investing. Begin by exploring resources like company annual reports and financial news websites. These sources provide invaluable insights into a company's performance and future prospects. When you analyze key financial metrics such as revenue growth and profit margins, you gain a clearer picture of a company's financial health. For instance, if a company's revenue has been consistently increasing over the years, it indicates strong business growth. Similarly, high-profit margins can suggest efficient operations and a competitive edge in the market.

To help you evaluate potential stocks, here's a detailed checklist of criteria to consider. First, look for companies with a strong track record of profitability and growth. This means examining their financial statements to see if they have been consistently profitable and if their earnings are growing. Next, consider the company's competitive position in its industry. Companies that dominate their markets or have a unique value proposition are often better investment choices.

Additionally, assess the company's management team. Experienced and capable leaders can significantly impact a company's success. Other factors to look at include the company's debt levels, cash flow, and future growth potential. By using this checklist, you can methodically evaluate each stock and make more informed decisions.

Blue-chip stocks are an excellent starting point for beginners. These are shares of large, reputable companies with a history of stable performance. Think of them as the "royalty" of the stock market. Blue-chip stocks are generally less volatile and offer more reliable returns, making them a relatively safe investment option. Companies like Apple, Microsoft, and Johnson & Johnson fall into this category. They have strong, established business models, consistent earnings, and are leaders in their respective industries. Investing in blue-chip stocks provides a solid foundation as you begin your investment journey, offering both stability and growth potential.

Diversification is another crucial aspect of building a robust investment portfolio. Diversifying your investments helps protect your portfolio from market volatility. By spreading your investments across different sectors, you reduce the impact of poor performance in any single sector. For instance, if you invest solely in technology stocks and the tech industry faces a downturn, your entire portfolio could suffer. However, if you also invest in sectors like healthcare, consumer goods, and finance, the impact of a downturn in one industry is mitigated by the performance of others. This balance can help you achieve more stable returns over time.

When selecting stocks, aim to invest in multiple sectors. The technology sector is often a favorite among young investors due to its growth potential and innovation. Companies like Google and Amazon are key players here. Healthcare is another essential sector, providing stable returns due to constant demand for medical services and products. Think of companies like Pfizer and Johnson & Johnson. Consumer goods, including companies like Procter & Gamble and Coca-Cola, offer steady returns as their products remain in demand regardless of economic conditions. By diversifying your investments across these sectors, you build a well-rounded portfolio that can weather various market conditions.

To further illustrate the importance of diversification, consider using a visual element like a pie chart to represent your diversified portfolio. This can help you visualize the allocation of your investments across different sectors and ensure that you are not overly concentrated in any one area.

Diversified Portfolio Example

Here is the pie chart representing the diversified portfolio allocation across different sectors. It visualizes the percentage distribution with Technology, Healthcare, Consumer Goods, Finance, Industrials, and Other sectors.

This allocation ensures that your portfolio is balanced and diversified, reducing your overall risk. Remember, diversification is not just about spreading your investments; it's about making strategic choices that align with your financial goals and risk tolerance. By carefully selecting stocks from various sectors and following a structured approach to research, you can build a resilient portfolio that stands the test of time.

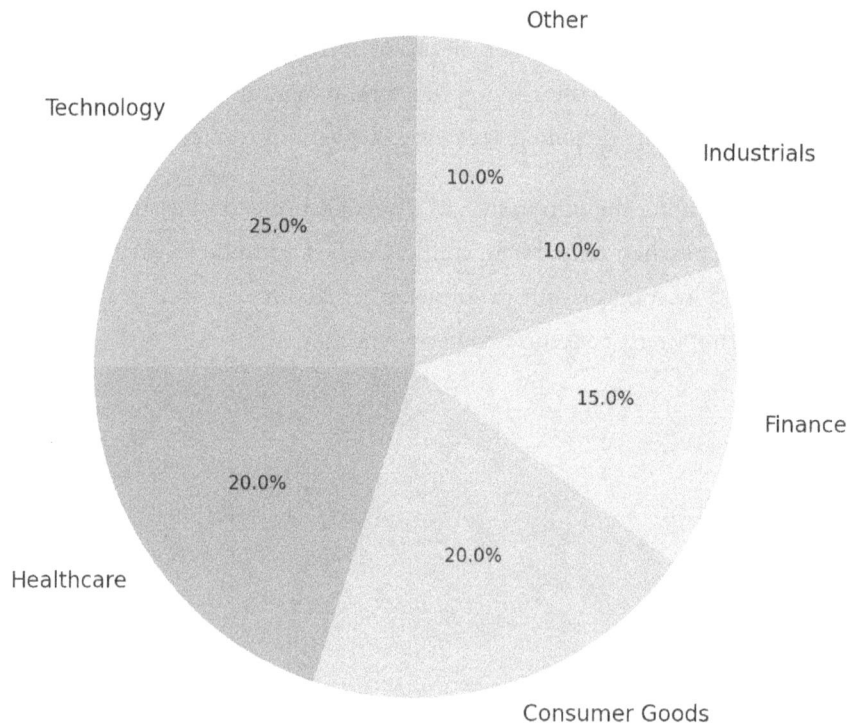

2.3 Budgeting for Investments: Allocating Money Wisely

Creating an investment budget might seem daunting at first, but it's an essential step in managing your finances effectively. Start by calculating your monthly income and expenses. List all your sources of income, including your salary, side gigs, and any other earnings. Next, jot down all your monthly expenses, from rent and utilities to groceries and entertainment. This exercise will give you a clear picture of your financial situation. Once you have a handle on your income and expenses, determine how much you can comfortably set aside for investments each month. Aim for an amount that doesn't strain your budget but still allows you to make meaningful progress toward your financial goals.

Before you dive into investing, it's crucial to have an emergency fund in place. An emergency fund acts as a financial safety net, ensuring you have the resources to cover unexpected expenses like medical bills or car repairs. This fund should be easily accessible, so it's best kept in a savings account. Aim to save at least three to six months' worth of living expenses. This cushion gives you peace of mind and prevents you from having to dip into your investments during emergencies. Building an emergency fund might take some time, but it's a vital step in securing your financial future. Once you have this fund in place, you can invest with greater confidence, knowing you have a backup plan.

There are several budgeting methods that can help you manage your finances effectively. One popular approach is the 50/30/20 rule. This rule allocates 50% of your income to needs, 30% to wants, and 20% to savings and investments. This method provides a balanced approach, ensuring you cover your essentials while still enjoying life and saving for the future. Another effective technique is zero-based budgeting, where every dollar is assigned a specific purpose. In this method, your income minus your expenses should equal zero. This approach forces you to account for every dollar, making it easier to identify areas where you can cut back and allocate more towards investments.

Maximizing your investment contributions can significantly boost your financial growth. Start by cutting unnecessary expenses. Small changes like dining out less frequently or canceling unused subscription services can free up additional funds for investing. Another effective strategy is to set up automatic transfers to your investment account. By automating your contributions, you remove the temptation to spend that money elsewhere. This consistent, hands-off approach ensures that you are steadily building your investment portfolio. Additionally, consider any windfalls, such as tax refunds or bonuses, as opportunities to make lump-sum contributions to your investments. These extra boosts can accelerate your progress towards your financial goals.

To put these budgeting strategies into practice, let's consider a simple exercise. Begin by tracking your income and expenses for one month. Use a spreadsheet or a budgeting app to categorize your spending and identify areas where you can cut back. Next, calculate how much you can realistically set aside for investments each month. Start with a small, manageable amount and gradually increase it as you become more comfortable with your budgeting. Use the table below to help you allocate your funds effectively and visualize your progress.

Monthly Budget Allocation

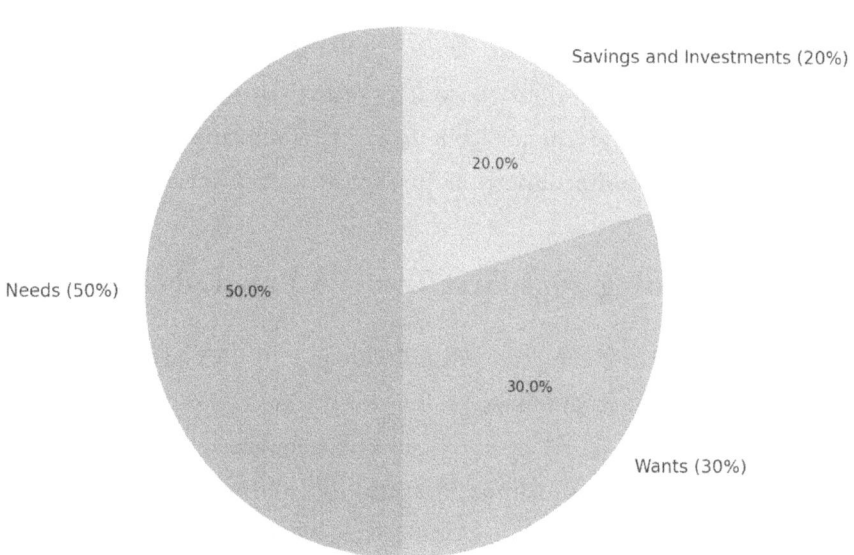

Here is the pie chart representing the monthly budget allocation. It shows the distribution of your income across needs, wants, and savings/investments.

Category Amount

- Income=$3,000

- Needs (50%)$1,500

- Wants (30%) $900

- Savings and Investments (20%) $600

By following this structured approach, you can create a realistic investment budget that aligns with your financial goals. Remember, budgeting is not a one-time task but an ongoing process. Regularly review and adjust your budget to ensure it continues to meet your needs and supports your investment objectives. With discipline and consistency, you can effectively manage your finances and make meaningful progress toward building your wealth.

Budgeting for investments is about making intelligent, intentional choices with your money. It requires discipline, planning, and a willingness to adjust your habits. By taking the time to create a budget, build an emergency fund, and maximize your investment contributions, you set yourself up for long-term financial success. These steps may seem small, but they are the foundation upon which you can build a robust investment portfolio and secure your financial future.

2.4 Opening Your First Trade: A Practical Guide

Opening your first trade might seem intimidating, but it's a straightforward process once you understand the steps. Imagine you're sitting at your computer, ready to take that leap. First, log in to your brokerage account. Navigate to the trading platform, which is usually prominently displayed on the main dashboard. You'll see options to buy or sell stocks. Click on the option to buy. Now, enter the stock ticker symbol of the company you wish to invest in. For example, if you want to invest in Apple, you'd enter "AAPL." Specify the number of shares or the dollar amount you want to invest. If you're buying fractional shares, you can invest as little as a few dollars. Double-check the details to ensure everything is correct, then click the button to place your order. This simple action is your entry into the world of investing.

Understanding the different types of orders is crucial for making informed trading decisions. A market order is the most straightforward type of order. When you place a market order, it executes immediately at the current market price. It is useful if you want to buy or sell a stock quickly, but be aware that the price you get might be slightly different from what you see on the screen due to market fluctuations. A limit order, on the other hand, allows you to set a specific price at which you're willing to buy or sell a stock. For instance, if a stock is currently trading at $50, but you only want to buy it if it drops to $45, you can set a limit order at $45. This type of order gives you more control over the price but may not execute if the stock never reaches your specified price. Other types of orders include stop orders and trailing stop orders, each serving different strategic purposes. Understanding these options helps you tailor your trading strategy to your financial goals and risk tolerance.

Before finalizing any trade, it's essential to review and confirm your order details. This step cannot be overstated. Ensure you have entered the correct stock ticker symbol and the right number of shares or dollar amount. Review the estimated cost, including any associated fees. Some brokerages charge small fees for transactions, which can add up over time. Double-checking these details can prevent costly mistakes. Imagine placing an order for 100 shares instead of 10 due to a typo—that could significantly impact your finances. Confirming your order details is a simple yet crucial step to ensure that your trades align with your investment strategy and budget.

After executing a trade, the work doesn't stop there. It's important to monitor the performance of your investments. Use your brokerage's portfolio tracker to keep an eye on how your stocks are doing. This tool provides real-time updates on the value of your portfolio and can help you make informed decisions about when to buy or sell. Setting up price alerts is another helpful feature. These alerts notify you of significant changes in the stock's value, helping you stay updated without constantly monitoring the market. If a stock's price hits a new high or drops to a level you're uncomfortable with, you'll receive an alert, allowing you to take timely action. This proactive approach helps you stay on top of your investments and make adjustments as needed to align with your financial goals.

Trading stocks is a dynamic process that requires attention and strategy. Each step, from choosing the correct order type to monitoring your investments post-trade, plays a vital role in your success as an investor. By understanding these steps and utilizing the tools available through your brokerage, you can navigate the trading process with confidence and precision.

2.5 Utilizing Investment Apps: The Best Tools for Millennials

Investing has never been more accessible, thanks to the rise of investment apps tailored to our digital age. Robinhood is a prime example, offering commission-free trading and an intuitive interface that makes it easy even for beginners to dive in. You can buy and sell stocks, ETFs, and even cryptocurrencies with just a few taps on your smartphone. Another popular app is Acorns, which rounds up your daily purchases and invests the spare change. This micro-investing approach is perfect for those who want to start small but build up their investment portfolio over time. For those looking for a bit more guidance, Betterment offers automated investing with personalized financial advice, ensuring that your portfolio aligns with your financial goals.

The advantages of using investment apps are numerous, particularly for millennials. Convenience is a significant factor; you can manage your investments on the go, whether you're commuting to work or lounging at home. These apps often come with low or no fees, making it more affordable to start investing. Many apps also offer educational resources to help you make informed decisions. For instance, some provide articles, video tutorials, and even interactive courses that cover everything from basic investing principles to advanced trading strategies. This wealth of information can empower you to become a more knowledgeable and confident investor, reducing the intimidation factor often associated with the stock market.

Choosing the right investment app depends on your individual needs and preferences. Start by considering the app's fee structure. Some apps offer commission-free trading, which can save you a lot of money in the long run. Next, look at the app's features. Does it offer robust research tools that can help you analyze stocks and make informed decisions? User-friendly interfaces are also crucial. An app with a cluttered or confusing design can hinder your investing experience. Additionally, consider whether the app offers features like automated investing or the ability to buy fractional shares. These features can make investing more accessible and less time-consuming.

To maximize the benefits of these investment apps, take full advantage of the features they offer. Automated investing options, for instance, can ensure that you consistently contribute to your investment portfolio without having to remember to do it manually. This "set it and forget it" approach can help you build wealth steadily over time. Many apps also offer tools to help you track your investments and analyze your portfolio's performance. Use these tools to stay informed about how your investments are doing and to make adjustments as needed. Educational resources provided by the app can also be invaluable. Spend some time exploring these materials to improve your financial literacy and make more informed investment choices.

In this chapter, we've covered the essential steps to get you started with investing. From the importance of starting small and selecting your first stocks to budget wisely and executing your first trade, each step builds your confidence and knowledge. Utilizing investment apps can further simplify and enhance your investing experience, making it more accessible and manageable. With these tools and strategies, you're well on your way to building a solid financial foundation. Next, we'll delve deeper into risk management and diversification, which are crucial aspects of maintaining a balanced and resilient investment portfolio.

Chapter 3
Risk Management and Diversification

"It's far better to buy a wonderful company at a fair price than a fair company at a wonderful price."

Warren Buffett

I remember a particular evening when I was just starting my investment path. I had placed all my savings into a single stock, convinced by a friend's sincere recommendation. For weeks, the stock climbed, and I felt like a financial genius. Then, almost overnight, it plummeted. Watching my hard-earned money evaporate was a harsh lesson in the importance of managing risk and diversifying investments. It was a wake-up call that underscored the inherent uncertainties in investing.

3.1 Understanding Risk: How to Assess and Manage It

Investment risk, at its core, refers to the possibility of losing some or all the money you invest. All investments come with a certain level of risk, but the key is to manage it effectively. Risk is an inherent part of the investment process, and understanding this can help you make more informed decisions. For instance, when you invest in stocks, you are exposed to market risk, which is the risk of losses due to factors that affect the entire market, such as economic downturns. This means that even if a company is performing well, its stock price can decline if the overall market is in a slump.

Apart from market risk, there are other types of investment risks you need to be aware of. Credit risk involves the possibility that a company may default on its debt obligations, which can be particularly relevant if you invest in bonds. If a company faces financial difficulties and cannot pay interest or repay the principal, you, as an investor, could face significant losses. Liquidity risk is another consideration. This is the risk of being unable to sell an investment at a fair price, potentially requiring you to accept a lower price or being unable to sell at all. For example, during times of financial crisis, it can be challenging to find buyers for certain assets, leading to liquidity issues.

Assessing your risk tolerance is a crucial step in managing investment risk. Your risk tolerance is influenced by several factors, including your investment timeline, financial goals, and ability to withstand market volatility. Start by considering how long you plan to invest. If you have a long-term horizon, you may be able to take on more risk as you have time to recover from potential losses. Conversely, if you need the money in a few years, a more conservative approach may be appropriate. Evaluate your financial goals. Are you investing for retirement, a home purchase, or simply to grow your wealth? Different goals may require different levels of risk. Additionally, think about your comfort level with market fluctuations. Some people can handle seeing their investments drop in value without panicking, while others may find it stressful. Use risk tolerance questionnaires available on financial websites and apps to get a clearer picture of your risk profile.

Managing investment risk involves several practical strategies. Diversification is one of the most effective ways to mitigate risk. By spreading your investments across different asset classes, such as stocks, bonds, and real estate, you can reduce your exposure to any single risk. For example, if you invest solely in technology stocks and the tech sector experiences a downturn, your entire portfolio could suffer. However, if you also invest in healthcare, consumer goods, and energy stocks, the impact of the tech downturn may be offset by gains in other sectors. This balanced approach helps stabilize your portfolio and provides more consistent returns over time.

Regularly reviewing and rebalancing your portfolio is another essential risk management strategy. Over time, the value of your investments will change, which can alter the balance of your portfolio. For instance, if your stocks perform exceptionally well, they may come to represent a more significant portion of your portfolio than intended, increasing your risk exposure. Periodically review your portfolio to ensure it remains aligned with your risk tolerance and investment goals. Rebalancing involves selling some of your overperforming assets and buying underperforming ones to restore your desired asset allocation. This disciplined approach helps maintain the balance between risk and return, ensuring your portfolio continues to meet your financial objectives.

Understanding and managing risk is not about avoiding risk altogether but about making informed choices that align with your financial goals and risk tolerance. By assessing your risk profile, diversifying your investments, and regularly reviewing your portfolio, you can navigate the uncertainties of the market with greater confidence and stability.

3.2 Diversification 101: Spreading Your Investments

Diversification is like not putting all your eggs in one basket. When you spread your investments across various assets, you reduce the impact of poor performance in any single investment on your overall portfolio. This strategy helps you achieve a more stable and resilient portfolio capable of withstanding market fluctuations. Imagine having all your money in one stock and that company faces a downturn. The loss can be devastating. But if you have investments spread across multiple sectors, the impact of one poor-performing stock on your entire portfolio is minimized.

There are several ways to diversify your investments effectively. Sector diversification involves spreading your investments across different industries, such as technology, healthcare, and finance. For instance, tech stocks might be booming, but healthcare stocks could provide stability during economic downturns. Another method is geographical diversification, which reduces risk by investing in markets from different regions and countries. This approach protects you from region-specific economic issues. For example, while the U.S. market might be facing challenges, emerging markets in Asia could be thriving, balancing your portfolio.

To diversify your portfolio effectively:

1. Start by assessing your current investments.

2. Identify any concentration of assets in a particular sector or region. If you notice that a significant portion of your portfolio is tied up in one area, it's time to spread your investments.

3. Allocate funds to different asset classes, such as stocks, bonds, and real estate.

Stocks can offer high returns but come with higher risk, while bonds provide more stability with lower returns. Real estate can add another layer of diversification, offering both income and potential appreciation. By balancing these asset classes, you can create a more resilient portfolio.

When diversifying, it's crucial to avoid common mistakes that can undermine your efforts. One such mistake is over-diversification, which can dilute potential returns and complicate portfolio management. While spreading your investments is good, holding too many assets can make it difficult to track and manage your portfolio effectively. Another pitfall is investing in highly correlated assets. For instance, if you invest in multiple tech stocks, they might all move in the same direction during market fluctuations. This correlation doesn't provide the desired diversification benefits. Instead, aim for a mix of assets that react differently to market conditions.

Diversification is not a one-time task but an ongoing process. As market conditions change and your investments grow, regularly review your portfolio to ensure it remains balanced. Rebalancing involves adjusting your asset allocation to maintain your desired level of diversification. For example, if your tech stocks have surged and now make up a significant portion of your portfolio, consider selling some and reallocating funds to underrepresented sectors like healthcare or bonds. This disciplined approach helps you maintain a balanced portfolio that aligns with your risk tolerance and financial goals.

Imagine you're building a team for a project. If everyone has the same skills, your team might struggle with challenges that require diverse expertise. Similarly, a well-diversified portfolio is like a well-rounded team capable of handling different market conditions. By spreading your investments across various assets, sectors, and regions, you create a robust portfolio that can weather the ups and downs of the market. This strategy not only reduces risk but also enhances your chances of achieving consistent, long-term returns.

3.3 Balancing Your Portfolio: Achieving the Right Mix

Asset allocation is the backbone of creating a balanced portfolio. It involves dividing your investments among different asset categories, such as stocks, bonds, and cash. This balance helps you achieve a mix that aligns with your risk tolerance and financial goals. Imagine asset allocation as a recipe; each ingredient contributes to the overall flavor. Stocks can offer high returns but come with higher risk, while bonds provide more stability and consistent income. Cash offers liquidity and security but low returns. The right mix of these assets can help you balance risk and return, ensuring your portfolio is both resilient and capable of growth.

There are various strategies to approach asset allocation, each tailored to different risk appetites and financial goals. A conservative strategy prioritizes capital preservation, involving a higher allocation to bonds and cash. This approach is suitable for those who want to minimize risk and protect their savings. For example, a conservative portfolio might consist of 60% bonds, 30% stocks, and 10% cash. On the other end of the spectrum, an aggressive strategy seeks higher returns with a higher allocation to stocks and other growth assets. This approach is suitable for younger investors with a longer investment horizon. An aggressive portfolio might consist of 80% stocks, 15% bonds, and 5% cash. A moderate strategy strikes a balance between risk and return, with a more even mix of stocks and bonds. This middle-ground approach might involve a portfolio of 50% stocks, 40% bonds, and 10% cash. Each of these strategies has its merits and is suited to different stages of life and financial goals.

Rebalancing your portfolio is crucial for maintaining your desired asset allocation. Over time, the value of your investments will change, causing your portfolio to drift from its target allocation. For instance, if your stocks perform exceptionally well, they may come to represent a more significant portion of your portfolio than intended, increasing your risk exposure. To rebalance:

1. Set a regular schedule, such as quarterly or annually, to review your portfolio.

2. During this review, assess each asset's performance and compare it to your target allocation.

3. If certain assets have grown beyond your target, sell a portion and reinvest the proceeds into underperforming assets to restore balance.

This disciplined approach ensures that your portfolio remains aligned with your risk tolerance and financial goals, helping you manage risk effectively.

Life changes can significantly impact your asset allocation decisions. Major events like marriage, buying a home, or retirement often require adjustments to your investment strategy. For example, as you approach retirement, you may want to shift towards a more conservative asset allocation to protect your savings from market volatility. This might involve increasing your allocation to bonds and reducing your exposure to stocks. If you receive a significant windfall, such as an inheritance or a bonus, consider how it fits into your overall investment strategy and adjust accordingly. You might want to use a portion of the windfall to diversify your portfolio further or to increase your allocation to safe, income-generating assets. These adjustments ensure that your portfolio continues to meet your evolving financial needs and goals.

Balancing your portfolio is not a one-time task but an ongoing process. As your financial situation and goals change, so too should your asset allocation. Regularly reviewing and adjusting your portfolio helps you stay on track and ensures that your investments continue to align with your risk tolerance and financial objectives. By understanding the principles of asset allocation and rebalancing, you can create a balanced portfolio that is both resilient and capable of achieving your long-term financial goals.

3.4 The Role of ETFs in Diversification: A Beginner's Guide

Exchange-Traded Funds, or ETFs, are a fantastic tool for diversification. Think of them as investment funds that trade on stock exchanges, much like individual stocks. What sets them apart is that they typically track the performance of a specific index, sector, or asset class. For instance, if you invest in an ETF that tracks the S&P 500, you're essentially investing in a fund that mirrors the performance of the 500 companies in that index. This built-in diversification makes ETFs a powerful way to spread risk across multiple assets without having to pick individual stocks or bonds.

One of the biggest advantages of investing in ETFs is their low cost. ETFs often have lower expense ratios compared to mutual funds, making them a cost-effective option for beginners. The expense ratio is the annual fee that all funds or ETFs charge their shareholders. It covers the operational costs of managing the fund. Lower fees mean more of your money stays invested, which can significantly impact your returns over time. Another benefit is the ease of trading. Since ETFs are traded on stock exchanges, you can buy and sell them just like you would with individual stocks. This liquidity allows for quick transactions, making it easier to manage your investments.

When selecting ETFs, you'll want to consider several criteria to ensure they align with your investment goals and risk tolerance. Start by looking for ETFs with low expense ratios. It minimizes costs and maximizes returns. High liquidity is also essential; it ensures you can buy and sell the ETF quickly without affecting its price. Next, examine the ETF's underlying index. Does it align with your investment objectives? For example, if you're interested in tech stocks, you might look for an ETF that tracks a technology index. Additionally, consider the ETF's performance history and how it has fared in different market conditions. That will give you a sense of its reliability and growth potential.

Incorporating ETFs into your diversified portfolio can be done in several ways. Broad-market ETFs are a great starting point for beginners. These ETFs give you exposure to the overall stock market, providing a solid foundation for your portfolio. For example, the Vanguard Total Stock Market ETF (VTI) offers exposure to the entire U.S. stock market, making it a popular choice for many investors. Sector-specific ETFs, on the other hand, allow you to target particular industries or themes. If you have strong convictions about the growth potential of a specific sector, such as healthcare or technology, you can invest in ETFs that focus solely on those areas.

Consider the strategy of using a mix of broad-market and sector-specific ETFs. This approach allows you to benefit from the stability of a diversified market exposure while also taking advantage of growth opportunities in specific sectors. For instance, you could allocate a portion of your portfolio to a broad-market ETF to cover the general economy and another portion to a tech-focused ETF to tap into technological advancements. This balanced approach helps you spread risk and capture growth across different areas.

Managing risk is crucial, especially when you have limited funds to invest. Smaller investors often have less capital to absorb losses, so effective risk management becomes even more critical. Implementing strategies to protect your investments and achieve steady growth should be a top priority. One practical tip is to consider investing in low-cost ETFs and mutual funds. These options provide broad exposure to different asset classes without requiring a significant upfront investment. For instance, you can gain access to a diversified portfolio of stocks, bonds, and other securities with just a small amount of money, reducing the risk associated with individual stock picking.

Another effective strategy is using fractional shares. This allows you to build a diversified portfolio with smaller amounts of money. Fractional shares let you invest in expensive stocks without needing to buy a whole share. For example, if you want to invest in Amazon but can't afford a full share, you can buy a fraction of it.

This way, you can diversify your investments across multiple high-quality stocks without needing a large sum of money. This approach democratizes investing, making it accessible to everyone, regardless of their financial situation.

Dollar-cost averaging is another powerful technique for managing risk and building wealth over time. This strategy involves investing a fixed amount of money at regular intervals, regardless of market conditions. By doing so, you buy more shares when prices are low and fewer shares when prices are high, which can lower your average cost per share over time. This method helps reduce the impact of market volatility and provides a disciplined approach to investing. It's particularly useful for those who may feel anxious about market fluctuations, as it removes the need to time the market.

Maintaining an emergency fund and ensuring liquidity in your portfolio are also essential risk management practices. An emergency fund acts as a financial safety net, allowing you to cover unexpected expenses without having to sell your investments at a loss. Aim to save at least three to six months' worth of living expenses in a liquid account, such as a savings account or money market fund. This cushion provides peace of mind and financial stability, enabling you to invest with confidence. Additionally, keeping a portion of your portfolio in liquid assets, such as cash or short-term bonds, ensures you have quick access to funds if needed. This flexibility allows you to navigate market downturns and unforeseen financial challenges more effectively.

3.5 Managing Risk on a Limited Budget: Practical Tips

When you have limited funds to invest, managing risk becomes even more crucial. Small investors often have less capital to absorb losses, making effective risk management strategies essential to protect your investments and achieve steady growth. Imagine putting your hard-earned money into a single stock that suddenly tanks; the impact can be devastating. So, what can you do to manage risk effectively while working with a smaller budget?

Diversifying on a budget is entirely possible with the right tools and strategies. Low-cost ETFs and mutual funds are excellent for gaining broad exposure to different asset classes without needing a large sum of money. These options allow you to invest in a diversified portfolio of stocks, bonds, or other securities, spreading your risk across multiple assets. Fractional shares are another fantastic way to diversify with limited funds. They enable you to buy a portion of high-priced stocks, allowing you to build a diversified portfolio without needing thousands of dollars. For instance, you could own a fraction of Apple, Google, and Amazon, thereby reducing your risk by not putting all your money into one company.

Dollar-cost averaging is a powerful strategy for managing risk and building wealth over time. This method involves investing a fixed amount of money at regular intervals, regardless of market conditions. By consistently investing, you buy more shares when prices are low and fewer shares when prices are high, which helps lower the average cost of your investments over time. This approach reduces the impact of market volatility and provides a disciplined way to build your portfolio. Imagine setting aside $50 every month and investing it in your chosen ETF or stock. Over time, this consistent investment can grow significantly, taking advantage of market dips and rises.

Maintaining an emergency fund and ensuring liquidity in your portfolio is also vital for managing risk. An emergency fund acts as a financial safety net, allowing you to cover unexpected expenses without having to sell your investments at a loss. This fund should be easily accessible and stored in a savings account or money market fund, providing you with immediate liquidity when needed. Aim to save at least three to six months' worth of living expenses. Keeping a portion of your portfolio in liquid assets, such as cash or short-term bonds, ensures you have quick access to funds if necessary. This flexibility allows you to navigate market downturns and unforeseen financial challenges more effectively, providing peace of mind and financial stability.

Imagine you're a student or a young professional just starting to invest. You might not have a lot of money to spare, but that doesn't mean you can't build a solid investment portfolio. By focusing on low-cost ETFs, utilizing fractional shares, and practicing dollar-cost averaging, you can create a diversified portfolio that grows steadily over time. Moreover, by maintaining an emergency fund and keeping some assets liquid, you ensure that you're prepared for unexpected expenses, allowing you to invest with greater confidence.

Managing risk on a limited budget requires a thoughtful and disciplined approach. By diversifying your investments, practicing dollar-cost averaging, and maintaining an emergency fund, you can build a resilient portfolio capable of weathering market fluctuations. These strategies not only protect your investments but also set the stage for steady, long-term growth, providing a solid foundation for your financial future.

This chapter has explored the intricacies of risk management and diversification, providing you with the tools to build a resilient portfolio. As we move forward, we'll delve into analyzing stocks and making informed investment decisions, further enhancing your ability to navigate the stock market successfully.

Chapter 4

Analyzing Stocks and Making Decisions

"Given a 10% chance of a 100 times payoff, you should take that bet every time."

Jeff Bezos

I remember the first time I decided to dig deep into a company's financial statements. It felt like deciphering an ancient language. I had just bought a few shares of a tech startup based on a friend's recommendation. The stock had been performing well, but I wanted to understand why.

Armed with a cup of coffee and my laptop, I began to explore the company's financial health. Within a few hours, I realized how much financial statements could reveal about a company's journey, its strengths, weaknesses, and future potential. That experience transformed me from a casual investor to someone who understood the importance of informed decisions.

4.1 Reading Financial Statements: The Basics

Understanding financial statements is like having a map that guides you through the financial landscape of a company. There are three main financial statements you need to familiarize yourself with: the income statement, the balance sheet, and the cash flow statement. Each of these documents offers unique insights into different aspects of a company's financial health, helping you make more informed investment decisions.

The income statement, often referred to as the profit and loss statement, provides a summary of a company's revenue and expenses over a specific period. It shows how the company performed financially during that time. Key components of the income statement include revenue, cost of goods sold (COGS), and net income. Revenue represents the total amount of money earned from sales. For instance, if a company sells $1 million worth of products in a quarter, that figure appears under revenue. The cost of goods sold includes all the direct costs associated with producing those goods. Subtracting COGS from revenue gives you the gross profit, which indicates how efficiently a company produces its goods. Finally, net income, also known as profit, is the amount remaining after all expenses, including operating costs and taxes, are subtracted from the revenue. This bottom-line figure tells you how much profit the company made during the reporting period.

The balance sheet, on the other hand, provides a snapshot of a company's financial condition at a specific point in time. It lists the company's assets, liabilities, and shareholders' equity. Think of assets as everything the company owns that has value, including cash, inventory, and property. Liabilities are what the company owes, such as loans and accounts payable. Shareholders' equity represents the net worth of the company, which belongs to the shareholders. The balance sheet follows the accounting equation: Assets = Liabilities + Shareholders' Equity. This equation ensures that the company's finances are in balance. For example, if a company has $500,000 in assets and $300,000 in liabilities, the shareholders' equity would be $200,000. Understanding the balance sheet helps you assess the company's financial stability and how well it can meet its obligations.

The cash flow statement tracks the flow of cash in and out of the business over a specific period. It is divided into three sections: operating activities, investing activities, and financing activities. Operating activities include cash generated from the company's core business operations. For instance, cash received from customers and cash paid to suppliers fall under this category. Investing activities involve cash spent on or received from investments in assets or securities. This could include purchasing new equipment or selling an old asset. Financing activities cover cash flows related to borrowing and repaying debt, issuing stock, and paying dividends. By examining the cash flow statement, you can determine how well a company manages its cash and whether it generates enough cash to support its operations and growth.

To help you get started, here's a quick exercise. Choose a company you are interested in and find its latest financial statements online. Take some time to explore each statement and identify the key components we've discussed. Note down the revenue, net income, total assets, liabilities, and cash flows from operating activities. This exercise will give you a hands-on understanding of how to read financial statements and what to look for when analyzing a company's financial health.

Financial Statement Analysis Exercise

1. Choose a company and locate its latest financial statements.

2. Identify and note down the following:

    - Revenue

    - Net income

    - Total assets

    - Total liabilities

    - Cash flows from operating activities

By regularly practicing this exercise, you'll become more comfortable with financial statements and better equipped to evaluate companies for potential investment. Understanding these documents is a critical skill that will serve you well as you navigate the stock market and make informed investment decisions.

4.2 Key Indicators to Watch: What Really Matters

When analyzing stocks, key financial ratios serve as vital tools to gauge a company's performance and financial health. The Price-to-Earnings (P/E) ratio is one of the most commonly used metrics. It compares a company's current share price to its earnings per share (EPS). For example, if a company's stock is trading at $50 and its EPS is $5, the P/E ratio is 10. It means investors are willing to pay $10 for every $1 of earnings. A high P/E ratio might indicate that the stock is overvalued, or it could mean that investors expect high growth in the future. Conversely, a low P/E ratio might suggest that the stock is undervalued or that the company is facing challenges.

Another important ratio is the Debt-to-Equity ratio, which measures a company's financial leverage by comparing its total liabilities to shareholders' equity. For instance, if a company has $100 million in liabilities and $50 million in equity, its Debt-to-Equity ratio would be 2.0. This ratio indicates how much debt the company is using to finance its operations relative to its equity. A higher ratio means more debt, which can be risky if the company faces financial difficulties. On the other hand, a lower ratio suggests that the company is less reliant on borrowing and may be in a more stable financial position.

Return on Equity (ROE) is another critical metric that investors use to assess a company's profitability. It measures how effectively a company is using its equity to generate profit. To calculate ROE, you divide the company's net income by its shareholders' equity. For example, if a company has a net income of $10 million and equity of $50 million, the ROE would be 20%. That means the company generates a 20% return on every dollar of equity. A high ROE indicates efficient management and strong profitability, making the company an attractive investment.

Quarterly earnings reports are essential for evaluating a company's performance. These reports provide insights into a company's profitability and future outlook. They include vital metrics such as revenue, net income, and EPS, offering a snapshot of the company's financial health. When analyzing earnings reports, look for trends in revenue and earnings growth over multiple quarters. Consistent growth can indicate a strong, stable company. For instance, if a company shows steady revenue increases over several quarters, it suggests that its products or services are in demand. Conversely, declining earnings can be a red flag, signaling potential problems.

Dividend yield is a crucial indicator for assessing the attractiveness of dividend-paying stocks. It is calculated by dividing the annual dividend payment by the stock's current price. For example, if a stock is priced at $100 and pays an annual dividend of $4, the dividend yield is 4%. A higher dividend yield can indicate a more attractive income-generating investment, especially for those looking for regular income from their portfolio. However, it's essential to ensure that the company can sustain its dividend payments. High yields might sometimes be a sign of trouble if the company's stock price has fallen significantly.

Market capitalization, or market cap, helps investors understand a company's size and stability. It is calculated by multiplying the current stock price by the total number of outstanding shares. Large-cap stocks, generally those with a market cap over $10 billion, are usually more stable but offer slower growth. They are often established companies with a long track record of performance. Small-cap stocks, on the other hand, have a market cap of less than $2 billion and can provide higher growth potential but come with higher risk. These companies are often in the early stages of growth, which can lead to more significant gains but also increased volatility.

Understanding these key indicators can significantly enhance your ability to analyze stocks and make informed investment decisions. Financial ratios like the P/E ratio, Debt-to-Equity ratio, and ROE provide valuable insights into a company's valuation, leverage, and profitability. Earnings reports offer a regular check-up on a company's performance, while dividend yield helps assess the income potential of dividend-paying stocks. Lastly, market cap gives you a sense of a company's size and stability, helping you build a balanced portfolio tailored to your risk tolerance and financial goals. By mastering these indicators, you'll be well-equipped to navigate the stock market and make decisions that align with your investment strategy.

4.3 Understanding Market Trends: Decoding the Signals

Market trends are the general direction in which the market is moving, either upward (bullish) or downward (bearish). Recognizing these trends is crucial for making informed investment decisions. When the market is bullish, stock prices are generally rising, driven by strong demand and positive investor sentiment. Conversely, a bearish market signals falling prices, often due to economic downturns or negative market sentiment. Understanding whether the market is trending up or down can help you decide when to buy or sell stocks.

Economic indicators play a significant role in shaping market trends. For instance, Gross Domestic Product (GDP) measures the total value of goods and services produced in a country, serving as a broad indicator of economic health. A rising GDP often indicates economic growth, which can positively impact stock prices. Conversely, a declining GDP might signal economic troubles, leading to a bearish market. Unemployment rates are another critical indicator. High unemployment suggests economic weakness, potentially dragging down stock prices.

On the other hand, low unemployment rates typically indicate a strong economy, boosting market confidence. Inflation, the rate at which prices for goods and services rise, also affects market trends. Moderate inflation can be a sign of a growing economy, but hyperinflation can erode purchasing power, negatively impacting stock prices.

Technical analysis tools are invaluable for identifying and understanding market trends. Moving averages, for example, smooth out price data to highlight trends over a specific period. A simple moving average (SMA) calculates the average stock price over a set number of days, providing a clearer view of the market's direction. The Relative Strength Index (RSI) measures the speed and change of price movements, helping identify overbought or oversold conditions. An RSI above

70 suggests a stock is overbought and might be due for a price correction, while an RSI below 30 indicates it might be oversold and could rebound. Bollinger Bands consist of a moving average and two standard deviations plotted above and below it, creating a band. These bands help you understand volatility, with prices often bouncing between the upper and lower bands. When prices break through these bands, it might signal a significant move.

Analyzing market trends requires a combination of tools and techniques. Start by examining historical price charts to identify long-term trends. Look for patterns that indicate whether the market is in a bullish or bearish phase. Combine multiple indicators to get a more comprehensive view of market conditions. For instance, use moving averages to identify the overall trend, RSI to gauge momentum, and Bollinger Bands to assess volatility. This multi-faceted approach provides a well-rounded understanding of market trends, helping you make more informed investment decisions.

When you look at historical price charts, you can spot long-term trends that offer valuable insights into market behavior. For example, a stock that has consistently trended upward over the past five years might indicate a strong, stable company. Conversely, a stock with erratic movements might signal volatility and higher risk. Combining these observations with technical indicators gives you a clearer picture of the market's direction. For instance, if the moving average is trending upward and the RSI is below 70, it might be a good time to buy.

Incorporating these tools into your analysis helps you navigate the complexities of the stock market. By understanding market trends and using technical analysis, you can make more informed decisions that align with your investment strategy. This knowledge empowers you to identify opportunities and manage risks effectively.

4.4 When to Buy and Sell: Timing Your Trades

Timing your trades is crucial for maximizing returns. Buying stocks at lower prices and selling them at higher prices can significantly impact your overall investment performance. However, it's easier said than done. The stock market is influenced by various factors, making it challenging to predict the perfect time to buy or sell. Avoiding emotional decisions is critical. When the market is volatile, it's easy to get caught up in the excitement or panic, leading to impulsive moves that can hurt your portfolio. Staying disciplined and sticking to a well-thought-out strategy can lead to more profitable trading. For instance, instead of buying a stock just because it's trending on social media, take the time to analyze its fundamentals and potential for growth.

Entry and exit points are critical in your trading strategy. Entry points are the optimal times to buy a stock, while exit points are the best times to sell. Identifying these points requires a combination of technical and fundamental analysis. Support and resistance levels are useful tools for this purpose. Support levels are price points where a stock tends to find buying interest, preventing it from falling further.

Conversely, resistance levels are points where selling pressure tends to prevent the stock from rising higher. By understanding these levels, you can make more informed decisions about when to enter or exit a trade. For example, if a stock is approaching a support level, it might be a good time to buy, as the price could potentially rebound from that point. On the other hand, if a stock is nearing a resistance level, it might be wise to sell before it faces significant selling pressure.

Stop-loss and take-profit orders are essential tools for managing risk and locking in profits. A stop-loss order automatically sells a stock when it reaches a specific price, limiting potential losses. For instance, if you buy a stock at $50 and set a stop-loss order at $45, the stock will be sold automatically if the price drops to $45, minimizing your losses. This strategy helps protect your investment from significant downturns. Take-profit orders work similarly but in the opposite direction. They sell a stock when it reaches a predetermined price, securing gains.

For example, if you set a take-profit order at $60 for a stock you bought at $50, the stock will be sold when it hits $60, ensuring you lock in your profits. These orders remove the emotional aspect of trading, helping you stick to your strategy and make more disciplined decisions.

Let's consider a case study of a successful trade. Imagine you identified a stock that was approaching its support level at $40. After conducting thorough research and analysis, you decided to buy the stock. Over the next few weeks, the stock price began to rise, eventually reaching its resistance level at $50. Recognizing this, you decided to sell the stock, locking in a 25% gain. This successful trade illustrates the importance of timing and the value of understanding support and resistance levels.

On the flip side, let's look at an unsuccessful trade where the investor failed to set a stop-loss order. Suppose you bought a stock at $70, confident in its growth potential. However, due to unforeseen market changes, the stock price began to decline rapidly. Without a stop-loss order in place, you watched the stock fall to $50, incurring significant losses. This scenario highlights the importance of using stop-loss orders to protect your investments from unexpected downturns.

Timing your trades requires a careful balance of analysis, strategy, and discipline. By understanding entry and exit points, utilizing stop-loss and take-profit orders, and learning from real-life examples, you can make more informed and profitable trading decisions. The stock market is unpredictable, but with the right tools and strategies, you can navigate it effectively and achieve your financial goals.

4.5 Real-Life Case Studies: Learning from Success and Failure

Understanding real-life case studies is like peering into the playbook of seasoned investors. They offer a treasure trove of practical lessons, helping you navigate the stock market's complexities. By analyzing both triumphs and setbacks, you gain a balanced perspective, enabling you to avoid common mistakes and replicate successful strategies. Imagine learning from someone who turned a modest investment into a fortune or from someone who lost it all due to a single oversight. These stories are not just about numbers; they are about the decisions, emotions, and strategies that shape investment outcomes.

One notable case study is the early investment in a tech startup that eventually grew into a major company. Think of the early backers of Amazon. In the 1990s, Amazon was just an online bookstore, but a few savvy investors saw the potential in Jeff Bezos's vision. They invested early, and as Amazon expanded into a global e-commerce giant, their investments grew exponentially. The strategy here was simple yet profound: identify a company with a strong vision and growth potential and invest early. These investors did their homework, believed in the company's long-term potential, and were rewarded handsomely for their foresight.

Another example is a long-term investment in a blue-chip stock that provided steady returns over the years. Consider the case of Coca-Cola. Investors who bought shares in Coca-Cola decades ago and held onto them have enjoyed consistent dividends and capital appreciation. The company's strong brand, global reach, and reliable revenue streams made it a stable investment. The lesson here is the value of patience and long-term planning. By investing in well-established companies with a proven track record, you can achieve steady, reliable returns. This approach requires discipline and a long-term perspective, but it can be incredibly rewarding.

On the flip side, there are cautionary tales of failed investments that highlight the importance of thorough research and risk management. One such case is the investment in a high-risk stock that failed due to poor financial management. Think of the Enron scandal. Investors were lured by the company's impressive growth and stock performance, but behind the scenes, Enron was engaged in fraudulent accounting practices. When the truth came out, the company's stock plummeted, and many investors lost their entire investment. This case underscores the importance of due diligence. Always dig deep into a company's financial health and management practices before investing.

Another example of a failed investment is a speculative investment that did not pay off. Consider the case of the dot-com bubble in the late 1990s and early 2000s. Many investors poured money into internet startups with little to no revenue, driven by the hype of the new digital age. When the bubble burst, these speculative stocks crashed, and investors faced significant losses. The lesson here is to avoid getting swept up in market hype. Focus on the fundamentals and ensure that the companies you invest in have solid financials and a viable business model.

From these case studies, several key takeaways emerge:

1. Diversification is crucial. Avoid putting all your money into one stock or sector. Spread your investments across different assets to mitigate risk.

2. Patience and long-term planning are invaluable. Investing in well-established companies and holding onto your investments can yield steady returns over time.

3. Thorough research is non-negotiable. Always conduct due diligence to understand a company's financial health and management practices.

4. Avoid speculative investments driven by market hype.

5. Stick to companies with solid fundamentals and a clear path to profitability.

By learning from both successful and failed investments, you can develop a more nuanced understanding of the stock market. These real-life examples provide practical lessons that can guide your investment decisions and help you build a resilient and profitable portfolio. As you continue your investment journey, remember these lessons and apply them to your strategy, ensuring a balanced and informed approach to stock market investing.

In this chapter, we've explored the fundamentals of stock analysis, from reading financial statements to understanding key indicators and market trends. By mastering these skills and learning from real-life case studies, you can make informed investment decisions and build a resilient portfolio. Next, we'll delve into advanced investment strategies that can further enhance your financial growth.

Chapter 5

Long-Term Investment Strategies

"Compound interest is the eighth wonder of the world. He who understands it, earns it; he who doesn't, pays it."

Albert Einstein

When I was in my mid-twenties, I had a conversation with a mentor that changed the way I thought about money. He asked me, "Do you know the most powerful force in the universe?" I guessed things like love, gravity, or even time. He smiled and shook his head. "It's compound interest." That simple statement opened my eyes to the concept that would become a cornerstone of my investment philosophy. The magic of compounding transformed my approach to saving and investing, and it's something I believe can do the same for you.

5.1 The Power of Compounding: Building Wealth Over Time

Compound interest is more than just a financial term; it's a powerful force that can significantly enhance your wealth. At its core, compound interest is the process where the value of an investment grows because the earnings on that investment—both capital gains and interest—earn interest as time passes. Imagine you invest $1,000 at an annual return of 5%. In the first year, your investment grows to $1,050. In the second year, you earn interest not only on the original $1,000 but also on the $50 earned the previous year, bringing your total to $1,102.50. This cycle continues, and with each passing year, your investment grows at an accelerating rate. This exponential growth is the essence of compounding.

To truly appreciate the impact of compounding over time, consider this: If you invest $100 per month at an annual return of 7%, your investment can grow to over $120,000 in 30 years. That's the power of small, consistent investments. Even a one-time investment can yield impressive results. For example, a one-time investment of $1,000 at the same 7% annual return would grow to nearly $7,612 in 30 years. These figures underscore the importance of consistency and patience in investing. The longer you allow your investments to compound, the more significant the growth.

Starting early is crucial for maximizing the benefits of compounding. The earlier you begin investing, the more time your money has to grow. For instance, starting to invest in your 20s can result in a significantly larger portfolio compared to starting in your 30s or 40s. The longer your money is invested, the more it can benefit from compound interest. Consider this: If you start investing $100 a month at age 25 and continue until age 65, you could accumulate over $240,000, assuming a 7% annual return. However, if you start at age 35 with the same monthly investment, you would only accumulate around $120,000 by age 65. The difference is stark and highlights the importance of starting early.

There are several practical strategies you can implement to maximize compound growth. One effective approach is to reinvest dividends and interest. When you receive dividends or interest payments from your investments, reinvesting them allows those payments to generate additional returns. This reinvestment accelerates the compounding effect, leading to greater overall growth. Many brokerage accounts offer automatic reinvestment options, making it easy to take advantage of this strategy. Additionally, maintaining a long-term perspective is vital. Avoid the temptation to withdraw funds prematurely, as this disrupts the compounding process. The longer you keep your money invested, the more it can grow.

Another strategy is to make regular contributions to your investment accounts. Consistency is key. By investing a fixed amount regularly, you take advantage of dollar-cost averaging, which can lower the average cost of your investments over time. This approach helps mitigate the impact of market volatility and ensures that you are continually contributing to your investment portfolio. Setting up automatic transfers from your bank account to your investment account can simplify this process and ensure that you remain disciplined in your investment efforts.

Consider incorporating a visual element to illustrate the power of compounding. A simple chart can vividly demonstrate how small, consistent investments grow exponentially over time, making the concept more tangible and relatable. This visual representation can serve as a powerful motivator, encouraging you to start investing early and consistently.

Compound Growth Example

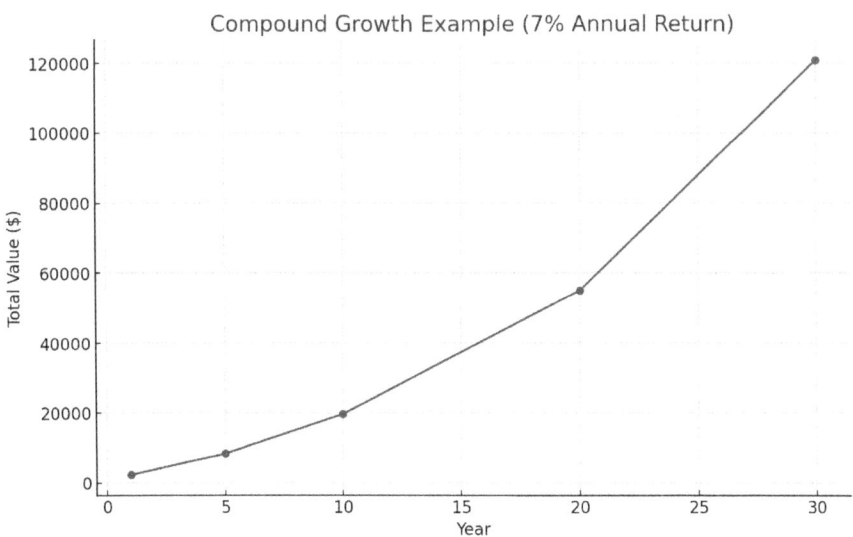

Here is the chart illustrating the compound growth of an investment with a $1,000 initial investment, $100 monthly contributions, and a 7% annual return over 30 years. The chart highlights the increasing total value at key points (1, 5, 10, 20, and 30 years).

This chart shows how your investments can grow over time with regular contributions and the power of compound interest. It highlights the importance of starting early, being consistent, and allowing your investments to grow uninterrupted.

Compound interest is a powerful tool for building long-term wealth. By understanding how compounding works, starting early, and implementing strategies to maximize growth, you can harness this force to achieve your financial goals. The key is to be patient, consistent, and disciplined, allowing time to work in your favor.

5.2 Planning for Retirement: Start Early, Finish Strong

Retirement planning is not just for those nearing the end of their careers; it's a crucial step you should take as early as possible. The sooner you start planning for retirement, the more time you have to build a substantial nest egg. It isn't just about saving money; it's about taking advantage of the growth that comes from long-term investments. When you start early, you not only have more years to contribute but also benefit from the compound growth of your investments. This combination can significantly enhance the size of your retirement fund, allowing you to retire comfortably and securely.

Retirement accounts are one of the most effective tools for building your retirement savings. A 401(k) is a popular choice, especially if your employer offers one. It's an employer-sponsored retirement plan that provides tax advantages and often includes matching contributions from your employer. This match is essentially free money added to your retirement fund, and it's crucial to take full advantage of it. On the other hand, an Individual Retirement Account (IRA) is another excellent option. Unlike a 401(k), an IRA is not tied to your employer, giving you more flexibility in terms of investment choices. A Roth IRA, in particular, is favored by many young investors because it allows for tax-free withdrawals in retirement. By paying taxes on your contributions now, you can enjoy tax-free growth and withdrawals later, which can be a significant benefit if you expect to be in a higher tax bracket when you retire.

Setting retirement goals can seem overwhelming, but breaking it down into manageable steps makes it more approachable. Start by envisioning the type of retirement you want. Consider factors like your desired lifestyle, where you want to live, and your health care needs. Calculate your expected retirement expenses based on these factors and your current lifestyle. This gives you a target to aim for. Next, determine how much you need to save annually to reach your retirement goals. Take into account factors like inflation and expected returns on your investments. Financial calculators can be incredibly helpful here, offering a realistic picture of what you need to save each year.

Maximizing your retirement savings involves several strategies. First, take full advantage of employer-matching contributions in your 401(k) plan. This match is essentially free money, and not contributing enough to get the full match is like leaving money on the table. If your employer matches 50% of your contributions up to 6% of your salary, aim to contribute at least 6%. Another effective strategy is to increase your contribution rate annually or whenever you receive a raise. This incremental approach can significantly boost your retirement savings over time without feeling like a huge sacrifice. Additionally, consider diversifying your investments to balance risk and return. A mix of stocks, bonds, and other assets can help protect your portfolio from market volatility while still providing growth.

To further enhance your retirement planning, consider using a step-by-step guide to set your goals and track your progress. Calculating your expected retirement expenses and determining your annual savings target are crucial steps. Once you have these figures, create a detailed plan outlining the steps needed to achieve your goals. Regularly review and adjust your strategy to stay on track and accommodate changes in your financial situation. This disciplined approach ensures that you remain focused and motivated, making it more likely that you will achieve your retirement goals.

Planning for retirement is a long-term endeavor that requires discipline, consistency, and strategic thinking. By starting early, taking advantage of various retirement accounts, and setting clear goals, you can build a substantial retirement fund that allows you to enjoy your golden years without financial stress. Regularly reviewing and adjusting your plan ensures that you stay on track, making it easier to achieve your retirement goals.

5.3 Dividend Stocks: The Benefits of Passive Income

Dividend stocks are an excellent way to create a steady flow of income. These are shares of companies that regularly distribute a portion of their profits to shareholders in the form of dividends. When you own dividend stocks, you receive payments, usually on a quarterly basis, simply for holding the shares. This passive income can be a reliable source of cash flow, especially during retirement or periods of market volatility. Companies that pay dividends are often financially stable and have a history of solid performance. For instance, firms like Procter & Gamble and Johnson & Johnson have been paying dividends for decades, showcasing their resilience and commitment to returning value to shareholders.

Investing in dividend stocks offers several advantages. One of the most appealing benefits is the consistent cash flow. Unlike growth stocks, where you might have to sell shares to realize gains, dividend stocks provide regular income without needing to liquidate your holdings. It can be particularly valuable during retirement when you might rely on this income to cover living expenses. Additionally, companies that pay dividends often have robust financial health. They generate enough profit to reward shareholders, which can be a sign of stability and reliability. Over time, the combination of steady income and potential capital appreciation can make dividend stocks an attractive addition to your portfolio.

Selecting high-quality dividend stocks requires a bit of research. Look for companies with a track record of consistent dividend payments and growth. A history of regular dividend increases often indicates a company's confidence in its financial stability. Consider the dividend yield, which is the annual dividend payment divided by the stock's current price. A higher yield can be attractive, but it's essential to ensure the dividend is sustainable. The payout ratio, which is the percentage of earnings paid out as dividends, is another crucial factor. A lower payout ratio suggests that the company retains enough earnings to invest in growth while still rewarding shareholders. Additionally, evaluate the company's overall financial health, including its earnings, debt levels, and cash flow. This holistic approach helps you identify companies that are likely to continue paying and increasing dividends.

Dividend reinvestment is a powerful strategy to accelerate portfolio growth. Instead of taking your dividends as cash, you can use them to purchase additional shares of the stock. This process is known as dividend reinvestment, and it compounds your investment over time. Many brokerages offer Dividend Reinvestment Plans (DRIPs) that automate this process, making it easy for you to reinvest dividends without extra effort. By reinvesting dividends, you increase the number of shares you own, which in turn generates more dividends. This cycle can significantly boost your portfolio's value over the long term, enhancing the compounding effect.

For instance, imagine you own shares in a company that pays an annual dividend of $2 per share. If you reinvest these dividends to buy more shares, your investment grows faster than if you took the dividends as cash. Over time, this reinvestment leads to owning more shares, which generate even more dividends. This compounding effect can turn a modest investment into a substantial portfolio. Many investors underestimate the power of reinvesting dividends, but it can be a game-changer for long-term wealth building.

To illustrate, consider this: Suppose you invest $10,000 in a dividend stock with a 4% yield. If you reinvest the dividends, the value of your investment can grow significantly more than if you took the dividends as cash. After 20 years, the difference in value can be substantial, thanks to the compounding effect of reinvested dividends. This strategy not only enhances your returns but also builds a more robust and resilient portfolio.

Dividend stocks offer a reliable source of passive income and potential for capital appreciation. By selecting high-quality dividend stocks, reinvesting dividends, and focusing on companies with strong financial health, you can create a portfolio that provides consistent income and grows over time. This approach aligns well with long-term investment strategies, allowing you to build wealth steadily and securely.

5.4 Setting Realistic Investment Goals: Your Financial Roadmap

Setting clear, realistic investment goals is crucial for successful investing. Having defined objectives gives you direction and motivation, helping you stay focused and disciplined. It's like planning a road trip: without a destination, you're just driving aimlessly. Investment goals provide that destination, guiding your financial decisions and actions. They help you prioritize and allocate resources effectively, ensuring that every dollar you invest has a purpose and contributes to your financial aspirations.

To set investment goals, begin by identifying your short-term, medium-term, and long-term objectives. Short-term goals might include saving for a vacation or emergency fund, typically achievable within a year or two. Medium-term goals could involve buying a car or saving for a down payment on a house, usually within three to five years. Long-term goals often encompass major life events like retirement or funding your child's education, which span over a decade. Each goal should be specific, measurable, achievable, relevant, and time-bound (SMART). For instance, instead of vaguely aiming to "save for retirement," set a goal to "save $500,000 for retirement by age 65."

Determine the amount of money needed for each goal and the timeline for achieving them. Break down these amounts into annual, monthly, or even weekly savings targets. This structured approach makes daunting financial goals more manageable. For example, if you need $20,000 for a home down payment in five years, you'd need to save $4,000 annually or roughly $333 monthly. Use financial calculators and tools to factor in inflation and expected returns, giving you a realistic picture of what's required. This clarity transforms abstract goals into actionable plans, making it easier to track your progress and stay motivated.

Achieving investment goals requires disciplined investing. Start by creating a detailed investment plan that outlines the steps needed to achieve each goal. This plan should include your target asset allocation, investment choices, and contribution schedule. Regularly review and adjust your strategy to stay on track and accommodate changes in your financial situation. Life is unpredictable; job changes, family commitments, and market fluctuations can impact your financial landscape. Being adaptable ensures your plan remains relevant and effective. For instance, if you receive a raise, consider increasing your savings rate to accelerate progress toward your goals.

Tracking progress is vital for staying aligned with your investment goals. Use financial tracking tools and software to monitor your investments, ensuring they are performing as expected and contributing towards your objectives. Many apps and platforms offer features to track your portfolio's value, returns, and allocation, providing real-time insights into your financial health. Set regular check-ins, such as quarterly or annual reviews, to assess progress and make necessary adjustments. These reviews are opportunities to celebrate milestones, identify areas for improvement, and recalibrate your strategy if needed. They keep you engaged and proactive, preventing complacency and ensuring continuous progress.

To help you stay organized and focused, consider creating a financial journal or checklist. Document your goals, action steps, and review dates. Reflect on your progress, challenges, and lessons learned. This practice not only keeps you accountable but also provides a tangible record of your financial journey, offering valuable insights and inspiration. You might include sections for goal setting, tracking progress, and periodic reflections. This structured approach ensures you remain committed and motivated, making it easier to achieve your financial aspirations.

Setting realistic investment goals is a foundational step in your financial journey. It provides direction, motivation, and a clear path toward your desired future. By defining and prioritizing your objectives, creating a detailed investment plan, and regularly tracking your progress, you can navigate the complexities of investing with confidence and clarity, steadily moving towards your financial goals without feeling overwhelmed or lost.

5.5 Building a Sustainable Portfolio: Ethical and Green Investments

Investing with a conscience isn't just a trend; it's a meaningful way to align your financial goals with your values. Ethical and sustainable investing involves selecting companies that prioritize environmental, social, and governance (ESG) factors. When you invest in ESG-focused companies, you're looking for businesses that are committed to reducing their carbon footprint, promoting fair labor practices, and maintaining transparent governance. Think of it as putting your money where your heart is, supporting firms that make a positive impact on society and the planet.

One of the compelling benefits of sustainable investing is that it allows you to contribute to positive social and environmental outcomes while potentially reaping financial rewards. Companies with strong ESG practices are often better positioned for long-term success and stability. For instance, businesses that invest in renewable energy and sustainable practices may be more resilient to regulatory changes and environmental risks. Additionally, firms that prioritize social responsibility and good governance can attract top talent, foster loyalty among customers, and build a strong reputation, all of which contribute to their financial performance.

When selecting ethical investments, there are several criteria to consider. Look for companies that provide transparent ESG reporting. This transparency allows you to assess their performance in critical areas such as carbon emissions, labor practices, and corporate governance. Companies with robust ESG reporting are often more committed to their sustainability goals and more accountable to their stakeholders. Another option is to consider ESG-focused mutual funds and ETFs. These funds invest in a diversified portfolio of companies that meet specific ESG criteria, offering you a convenient way to gain exposure to ethical investments without having to research each company individually.

Building a sustainable portfolio requires a balanced approach. Start by integrating ESG investments with traditional assets to achieve a well-rounded portfolio. Diversification remains crucial; even within ESG investments, it's essential to spread your risk across different sectors and asset classes. Regularly review and adjust your portfolio to ensure it continues to align with your values and financial goals. Market conditions and company practices can change, so staying informed and proactive is vital. This ongoing assessment helps you maintain a portfolio that reflects your ethical standards while also delivering financial returns.

To put these strategies into practice, consider setting up a periodic review schedule. Every quarter, assess your portfolio's alignment with your ESG criteria and make adjustments as needed. This could involve reallocating funds from companies that no longer meet your standards to those that do. Additionally, stay updated on the latest trends and developments in sustainable investing. Resources like ESG reports, sustainability indexes, and news on regulatory changes can provide valuable insights. By staying informed, you can make more educated decisions and keep your investments in line with your values.

For those looking to dive deeper into ethical and green investments, creating a checklist can be a helpful tool. This checklist might include assessing a company's ESG scores, reviewing their sustainability reports, and considering their impact on various social and environmental issues. By following a structured approach, you can systematically evaluate each potential investment and build a portfolio that aligns with your principles.

ESG Investment Checklist

- **ESG Scores:** Review the company's ESG scores from reputable rating agencies.

- **Sustainability Reports:** Read the company's latest sustainability reports.

- **Environmental Impact:** Assess the company's efforts to reduce its carbon footprint.

- **Social Responsibility:** Evaluate the company's labor practices and community involvement.

- **Governance:** Examine the company's governance structure and transparency.

Using this checklist can streamline your decision-making process, ensuring that your investments are both ethical and financially sound. It provides a clear framework for evaluating companies, making it easier to identify those that genuinely align with your values.

Building a sustainable portfolio is not only about making a positive impact but also about investing in companies poised for long-term success. By focusing on ESG factors, you can create a portfolio that reflects your values and contributes to a better world. As you integrate ethical investments into your strategy, remember to balance them with traditional assets and stay proactive in your reviews. This approach ensures that your portfolio remains aligned with your goals and adapts to changing market conditions.

By incorporating these principles into your investment strategy, you can build a portfolio that not only aims for financial growth but also supports positive societal and environmental changes. As you continue to learn and adapt, your investments can reflect not just your financial ambitions but also your commitment to a sustainable future.

Chapter 6
Avoiding Common Pitfalls

"The stock market is designed to transfer money from the Active to the Patient."

Warren Buffett

I remember the first time I let my emotions dictate my investment decisions. It was a bright Monday morning, and the market had just opened. The stocks I had carefully chosen and invested in started plummeting. My heart raced, my palms were sweaty, and panic set in. In a frenzy, I sold off my shares, locking in significant losses. Days later, the market rebounded, and I realized my mistake. This experience was a harsh lesson in the impact of emotional trading and the importance of maintaining a cool head.

6.1 Emotional Trading: Managing Your Psychology

Emotions can be a powerful force in investing, often leading to irrational decisions that can have lasting financial consequences. Fear and greed are the two primary emotions that can derail even the most well-thought-out investment strategies. Fear can grip you during market downturns, causing you to sell your investments at a loss, just as I did. The fear of losing more money often drives this reaction, but it can result in locking in losses that might have been temporary. On the other hand, greed can lead you to chase high-risk investments in the hope of quick gains. This mindset can push you to invest in volatile stocks without proper research, increasing the likelihood of significant losses.

Managing emotional trading requires a combination of strategies to help you stay calm and make rational decisions. One effective technique is to develop a clear investment plan and stick to it, regardless of market fluctuations. This plan should outline your investment goals, risk tolerance, and the types of assets you will invest in. By having a predefined strategy, you can make decisions based on logic rather than emotions. Additionally, using stop-loss orders can help limit potential losses and reduce emotional stress. These orders automatically sell a stock when it reaches a specific price, protecting your investments from significant downturns. For instance, setting a stop-loss order at 10% below your purchase price can prevent you from holding onto a losing investment for too long.

It's crucial to maintain a long-term perspective, focusing on your financial goals rather than short-term market movements. Market volatility is normal and often temporary. By staying focused on your long-term investment objectives, you can avoid reacting to daily market noise. For example, if your goal is to save for retirement, remember that short-term fluctuations are just small blips in your overall investment timeline. Keeping your eye on the bigger picture can help you stay calm during market turbulence and prevent impulsive decisions that could harm your long-term financial health.

Maintaining emotional discipline is essential for successful investing. Regularly review your investment plan and remind yourself of your goals. This practice can reinforce your commitment to your strategy and help you stay on track. Taking breaks from monitoring the market can also prevent anxiety and overtrading. Constantly checking stock prices can lead to stress and impulsive decisions. Instead, set specific times to review your portfolio, such as once a week or once a month. This approach allows you to make informed decisions without being overwhelmed by daily market movements.

Reflection Exercise: Emotional Check-In

Take a moment to reflect on your recent investment decisions. Think about a time when you made a decision based on emotions rather than logic. Write down the following:

1. What triggered your emotional response?

2. How did you feel at the time?

3. What was the outcome of your decision?

4. What could you have done differently to manage your emotions?

By regularly engaging in this exercise, you can become more aware of your emotional triggers and develop strategies to manage them effectively. Understanding your emotional patterns can help you make more rational investment decisions and improve your overall financial well-being.

6.2 The Danger of Overconfidence: Staying Humble

Overconfidence can be a silent killer in the world of investing. It often leads to excessive risk-taking and poor decision-making. You might find yourself believing you have a unique ability to predict market movements or pick the perfect stocks. This mindset often results in underestimating the risks involved and overestimating your own capabilities. For example, overconfident investors might pile into high-flying tech stocks, convinced they will continue to soar, only to watch them plummet during a market correction. This misjudgment can lead to significant financial losses and a bruised ego.

Humility in investing is not just a virtue; it's a necessity. Recognizing the limits of your knowledge can help you make more cautious and informed decisions. Acknowledging that you don't have all the answers opens the door to continuous learning and improvement. It encourages you to seek out information, ask questions, and consult with experts. Being open to learning from others can significantly enhance your investment strategy. For instance, listening to seasoned investors or financial advisors can provide valuable insights that you might not have considered. This approach fosters a mindset of growth and adaptability, which is crucial for long-term success.

Maintaining a balanced perspective can be challenging, especially when the market is performing well and your investments are yielding high returns. However, it's crucial to regularly review and analyze your past investment decisions to identify areas for improvement. This reflective practice can help you stay grounded and avoid the pitfalls of overconfidence. Additionally, seeking advice from experienced investors and financial advisors can provide a reality check. These experts can offer objective opinions and highlight potential risks that you might have overlooked. Engaging in discussions with them can broaden your perspective and help you make more balanced decisions.

Real-life examples illustrate the dangers of overconfidence vividly. Consider an investor who took on too much leverage, assuming the market would continue to rise. This person borrowed money to invest, expecting to amplify their returns. However, when the market turned, the losses were magnified, leading to significant financial distress. This scenario underscores the importance of understanding the risks associated with leverage and not assuming that markets will always move in your favor. Another case involves an investor who ignored diversification, believing they had identified the "perfect" stock. They invested heavily in one company, only to see it collapse due to unforeseen issues. This lack of diversification resulted in substantial losses, emphasizing the need for a balanced portfolio.

By understanding these risks and adopting strategies to stay humble, you can avoid the pitfalls of overconfidence. Regularly reviewing your investment decisions, seeking advice, and learning from others can help you maintain a balanced perspective and make more informed choices. This approach not only protects your investments but also fosters a mindset of continuous improvement and adaptability.

6.3 Avoiding the Herd Mentality: Thinking Independently

Herd mentality in investing can be a silent trap. It occurs when investors follow the crowd, often driven by fear or greed, without conducting their research. Picture this: a stock starts gaining popularity, and suddenly, everyone is buying in, convinced it will continue to rise. This phenomenon can lead to buying overvalued stocks, creating market bubbles. When the bubble bursts, those who follow the herd can experience significant losses. The fear of missing out (FOMO) can be powerful, but it's crucial to remember that not all widely touted investments are sound.

Following the crowd can also lead to selling during market panics. When a stock's price starts to drop, panic can set in. Investors, seeing others sell, often follow suit to avoid further losses. This herd behavior can lock in losses and prevent you from benefiting from subsequent recoveries. For instance, during market downturns, selling in a panic can mean missing out on potential rebounds when the market stabilizes. Instead of making decisions based on the actions of others, it's vital to conduct your own analysis and stick to your investment plan, even when the market is turbulent.

To make independent, well-informed investment decisions, thorough research and analysis are paramount. Start by evaluating the fundamentals of the company you're considering. Look into its financial health, market position, and future growth prospects. This approach helps you build a personal investment thesis based on your goals and risk tolerance. Developing this thesis involves asking critical questions: Does the company have a sustainable competitive advantage? Is its financial health robust? Does its business model align with long-term trends? By answering these questions, you ground your decisions in solid research rather than market hype.

Successful independent investors often stand out by sticking to their principles in the face of market trends. Consider the case of an investor who avoided the tech bubble by adhering to value investing principles. While many flocked to tech stocks in the late 1990s, this investor stayed away from overvalued companies with no clear path to profitability. When the bubble burst, they avoided the significant losses that many others faced. Their independent thinking and commitment to value investing principles paid off, highlighting the importance of sticking to your investment philosophy, even when it goes against the grain.

Another example is an investor who profited from a contrarian approach during a market downturn. When the market was bearish and most investors were selling, this individual saw an opportunity. They identified fundamentally strong companies that were undervalued due to market panic. By investing in these companies when others were fearful, they capitalized on the eventual market recovery. This contrarian strategy requires courage and conviction but can lead to substantial gains. It demonstrates the value of independent thinking and the rewards that can come from swimming against the tide.

Interactive Element: Independent Thinking Exercise

Take a moment to reflect on your recent investment decisions. Think about a time when you followed the crowd and a time when you made an independent decision. Write down the following:

1. What influenced your decision to follow the crowd?

2. What was the outcome of that decision?

3. What research or analysis did you conduct when making an independent decision?

4. How did that independent decision turn out?

By regularly engaging in this exercise, you can become more conscious of your decision-making process and strengthen your ability to think independently. Understanding the factors that influence your investments can help you make more rational and informed choices in the future.

6.4 Understanding Fees and Commissions: Keeping Costs Low

When I first started investing, I was so focused on picking the right stocks that I overlooked the impact of fees and commissions. It wasn't until I reviewed my year-end statements that I realized how much those small fees had chipped away at my returns. Even seemingly insignificant fees can add up over time, significantly reducing your overall gains. For instance, a $10 trading fee might not seem like much, but if you trade frequently, these costs can erode your investment returns. Understanding fee structures is crucial for maximizing your investment gains and ensuring that more of your money works for you.

Different types of fees and commissions can catch you off guard if you're not familiar with them. Trading fees are one of the most common costs charged by brokerages every time you buy or sell securities. These fees can vary widely, from a few dollars per trade on discount platforms to higher charges on full-service brokerages. Management fees are another common cost, especially if you invest in mutual funds or ETFs. These fees, often expressed as a percentage of your assets under management, cover the fund's operational costs. For example, a mutual fund might charge a 1% management fee, which can eat into your returns over time. Expense ratios are similar, representing the annual cost of owning an ETF or mutual fund. A high expense ratio can significantly impact your investment's growth, especially over the long term.

Minimizing fees and commissions is essential for maximizing your investment returns. One effective strategy is to choose brokerages that offer low or no commission fees for trading. Many online brokerages, like Robinhood and Charles Schwab, provide commission-free trades, making it cheaper to buy and sell stocks. Another approach is to opt for low-cost index funds and ETFs with low expense ratios. Funds like Vanguard's Total Stock Market ETF (VTI) often have expense ratios as low as 0.03%, making them cost-effective choices for long-term investors. Additionally, consider no-load mutual funds that do not charge a sales commission, allowing more of your money to be invested rather than going toward fees.

Transparency in fee structures is critical to understanding the actual cost of your investments. Always read the fine print and ask questions to ensure you fully understand all fees and charges associated with your investments. For instance, some brokerages might advertise low trading fees but have hidden costs like account maintenance fees or inactivity fees. Using fee comparison tools available on financial websites can help you evaluate different brokerages and funds, ensuring you make informed choices. Websites like Investopedia and NerdWallet offer comprehensive comparisons, making it easier to find the most cost-effective options.

When I started paying closer attention to fees, I made a concerted effort to switch to low-cost investments and transparent brokerages. It made a noticeable difference in my returns. For example, switching from a mutual fund with a 1% management fee to an ETF with a 0.03% expense ratio significantly boosted my investment growth over time. By keeping costs low, more of your money remains invested, compounding over the years and helping you achieve your financial goals faster.

Understanding and managing fees and commissions is an often-overlooked aspect of investing, but it's crucial for maximizing your returns. By choosing low-cost investments, seeking transparent fee structures, and being mindful of hidden charges, you can ensure that more of your hard-earned money works for you. This approach not only boosts your returns but also provides peace of mind, knowing that you're making the most of your investment opportunities.

6.5 The Risks of Day Trading: Why Patience Pays

Day trading is a high-stakes game where traders buy and sell securities within the same trading day, aiming to profit from short-term price movements. Unlike long-term investing, which focuses on holding assets for years, day trading is all about capitalizing on daily market fluctuations. This fast-paced approach requires constant monitoring of the market, making it both time-consuming and stressful. Imagine sitting in front of your computer screen, tracking every tick of the stock prices, and making rapid decisions based on fleeting information. The goal is to buy low and sell high within hours or even minutes, hoping to make quick profits. However, this strategy is fraught with complexities and risks that can easily outweigh the potential rewards.

The volatility inherent in day trading is one of its most significant challenges. Stock prices can swing wildly within a single day, influenced by various factors such as news events, economic data, and market sentiment. This unpredictability makes it difficult to consistently make profitable trades. Additionally, the high frequency of trading leads to substantial fees and commissions, which can quickly eat into your profits. Even with commission-free trading platforms, other costs like the bid-ask spread and slippage can add up. The need for constant vigilance and quick decision-making can also take an emotional toll, leading to stress and burnout. Unlike long-term investors who can afford to ride out market fluctuations, day traders must stay glued to their screens, ready to act at a moment's notice.

Real-life examples highlight the pitfalls of day trading. Consider the case of a day trader who over-leveraged, borrowing money to amplify their trades. When the market turned against them, the losses were magnified, leading to financial ruin. This scenario underscores the risks of using leverage without a solid risk management strategy. Another example involves a trader who relied heavily on emotional decision-making. Instead of sticking to a well-thought-out plan, they chased after stocks based on hunches and hype. Unsurprisingly, this approach led to significant losses. These examples serve as cautionary tales, illustrating how the allure of quick profits can blind traders to the inherent risks of day trading.

In contrast, a long-term investment approach offers several advantages that make it a safer and more sustainable strategy. One of the most significant benefits is the power of compounding. By holding investments over the long term, you allow your profits to generate their profits, leading to exponential growth. This compounding effect can significantly enhance your returns over time. Additionally, long-term investing reduces the impact of market volatility. While day traders must navigate daily price swings, long-term investors can afford to ignore short-term fluctuations. This stability allows you to focus on your financial goals without the constant pressure to act.

A disciplined, long-term approach can lead to more stable and consistent returns. By investing in fundamentally strong companies and holding them for years, you benefit from their growth and profitability. Long-term investing also aligns with a more relaxed lifestyle, free from the stress and anxiety of daily trading. Instead of spending hours glued to market charts, you can enjoy your day knowing that your investments are working for you in the background. This approach not only enhances your financial well-being but also contributes to a more balanced and fulfilling life.

To illustrate the benefits of long-term investing, consider the example of an investor who bought shares of a strong, established company like Microsoft or Apple and held onto them for decades. Over the years, these companies have grown, innovated, and rewarded their shareholders with substantial returns. This investor has benefited from the company's growth, dividends, and the compounding effect, achieving financial success without the stress and risks associated with day trading. This example underscores the value of patience and a long-term perspective in building wealth.

In summary, while day trading might seem exciting with the promise of quick profits, it comes with significant risks and challenges. Volatility, high costs, and emotional stress can easily outweigh the potential rewards. On the other hand, a long-term investment approach offers stability, the power of compounding, and the peace of mind that comes with focusing on long-term goals. By choosing patience over the allure of quick gains, you can build a more secure and prosperous financial future.

Chapter 7

Continuous Learning and Improvement

"Live as if you were to die tomorrow. Learn as if you were to live forever."

Warren Buffett

7.1 Essential Financial News Sources: Staying Informed

The first time I realized the importance of staying informed was during the 2008 financial crisis. I remember watching the news in disbelief as markets plummeted and companies I had invested in faced turmoil. It was a wake-up call. I understood that to navigate the stock market effectively; I needed to keep a pulse on financial news. This chapter aims to guide you in integrating financial news into your daily routine, ensuring you're always informed and ready to make well-grounded investment decisions.

One of the most reliable sources for comprehensive coverage of financial markets is The Wall Street Journal. Known for its in-depth analysis and timely reports, it provides a broad spectrum of information on global financial markets, economic news, and industry trends. Whether you're interested in the latest stock movements or policy changes affecting the economy, The Wall Street Journal covers it all. Another indispensable resource is Bloomberg, which offers real-time data and market analysis. Bloomberg's detailed reports and expert commentary make it a go-to for investors looking to understand market dynamics and anticipate future trends. Their financial news spans everything from corporate earnings to geopolitical developments, helping you stay ahead of the curve.

Staying informed is crucial for making sound investment decisions. When you regularly follow financial news, you gain insights into market trends and potential investment opportunities. For example, understanding economic indicators like GDP growth or unemployment rates can help you predict market movements and adjust your investment strategy accordingly. If you know that a weak jobs report has led to a rally in Treasuries and the Yen, you can anticipate the Federal Reserve's actions and position your investments advantageously. Moreover, being informed allows you to react promptly to market changes. Suppose you read about a major acquisition or a new regulatory policy affecting a sector you're invested in; this knowledge enables you to make timely decisions, whether it's buying, selling, or holding your positions.

Integrating news consumption into your daily routine doesn't have to be overwhelming. Start by setting aside a specific time each morning to catch up on financial news. This habit ensures you stay updated on market developments without feeling inundated. Use news aggregator apps like Feedly to curate and organize news from multiple sources. These apps allow you to customize your news feed, focusing on topics and industries that matter most to your investment strategy. By spending just 15-20 minutes each day reading curated news, you can stay informed without sacrificing too much of your time. Another practical tip is to listen to financial news podcasts during your commute or workout sessions. This multitasking approach helps you absorb valuable information while going about your daily activities.

Financial newsletters and blogs are also valuable resources for staying informed. Subscribing to reputable financial newsletters can provide you with concise and engaging summaries of the day's most important news. Morning Brew, for instance, offers a daily digest of financial news, making it easy to stay updated without spending hours sifting through articles. Its conversational tone and succinct format make complex topics accessible and engaging. The Motley Fool is another excellent resource, offering investment advice and stock recommendations through its newsletters. By subscribing to these newsletters, you gain access to expert insights and actionable tips, helping you make informed investment decisions. Blogs like Seeking Alpha and Investopedia provide in-depth articles and analysis on various financial topics, from stock market trends to investment strategies, adding another layer of knowledge to your investment toolkit.

Incorporating these resources into your daily routine can significantly enhance your financial literacy and investment insight. By staying informed, you equip yourself with the knowledge needed to navigate the stock market confidently and make well-grounded decisions. This proactive approach to learning fosters a deeper understanding of market dynamics, helping you stay ahead in your investment journey. As you continue to engage with these resources, you'll find yourself more adept at analyzing market trends, identifying investment opportunities, and reacting promptly to market changes, ultimately leading to better investment outcomes.

7.2 Recommended Books and Podcasts: Deepening Your Knowledge

When I first started investing, the deluge of information was overwhelming. Seeking guidance, I turned to books and podcasts, which became invaluable resources. One of the most influential books I read was "The Intelligent Investor" by Benjamin Graham. This classic guide to value investing lays out principles that have stood the test of time. Graham's insights into analyzing stocks and understanding market behavior provide a solid foundation for any investor. Another game-changer was "Rich Dad Poor Dad" by Robert Kiyosaki. This book dives into the fundamentals of financial literacy and wealth-building, emphasizing the importance of investing in assets that generate cash flow and equity value. Kiyosaki's narrative, comparing the financial wisdom of his two "dads," offers practical advice that is easy to understand and apply.

For those interested in a broader historical perspective, "The Ascent of Money" by Niall Ferguson is a must-read. This book traces the evolution of finance from ancient times to the present, providing context for modern financial systems and investment strategies. Ferguson's engaging storytelling makes complex financial concepts accessible and interesting. Another essential read is "The Little Book of Common Sense Investing" by John C. Bogle. Bogle, the founder of Vanguard Group, advocates for owning a diversified stock portfolio and holding it for the long term. His straightforward approach demystifies the investment process and underscores the benefits of low-cost index funds. These books, among others, have shaped my understanding of investing and can provide you with the knowledge to make informed decisions.

Podcasts have become a convenient and effective way to learn about investing, especially for those with busy schedules. They allow you to absorb valuable information while commuting, exercising, or doing household chores. One podcast that has consistently provided practical advice is "The Dave Ramsey Show." Ramsey offers insights on personal finance and debt management, helping listeners navigate financial challenges with confidence. His straightforward, no-nonsense approach makes complex financial topics easy to grasp. Another favorite is "How to Money," hosted by Joel and Matt. This podcast focuses on everyday financial topics and investment strategies specifically geared towards millennials. The hosts' relatable and engaging style makes learning about money management both enjoyable and informative.

For a deeper dive into investment strategies, "Invest Like the Best" with Patrick O'Shaughnessy is a treasure trove of knowledge. Each episode features interviews with successful investors, providing practical advice and inspiration. The guests share their unique perspectives on various investment approaches, from value investing to venture capital, offering listeners a wealth of actionable insights. Another excellent podcast is "The Motley Fool Money," which covers weekly financial news, stock market trends, and investment tips. The hosts' witty banter and expert analysis make it a fun and enlightening listen. These podcasts can help you stay updated on market trends, learn from industry experts, and refine your investment strategies.

To maximize your learning from books and podcasts, consider a few practical strategies. Taking notes while reading or listening can help you highlight key concepts and actionable advice. Jot down important points, quotes, and ideas that resonate with you. This practice not only reinforces your understanding but also creates a valuable reference for future use. Discussing insights with peers or in online forums can deepen your understanding and provide different perspectives. Engaging in conversations about what you've learned can clarify concepts and spark new ideas. Joining online communities like Reddit's r/investing or financial groups on social media platforms can connect you with like-minded individuals and experts, fostering a collaborative learning environment.

Additionally, setting specific learning goals can enhance your focus and motivation. For example, aim to read one investment book per month or listen to a podcast episode during your daily commute. Consistency is critical to building your financial knowledge over time. If you find a particular book or podcast episode especially impactful, consider revisiting it periodically to reinforce your learning. Creating a summary of the key takeaways and how you plan to apply them can also be beneficial. This reflective practice helps solidify your understanding and translates knowledge into actionable steps.

Incorporating these resources into your routine can significantly enhance your financial literacy and investment skills. By consistently engaging with books and podcasts, you stay informed, broaden your perspective, and make more educated investment decisions. This continuous learning approach empowers you to navigate the complexities of the stock market with confidence, ultimately leading to better financial outcomes.

7.3 Online Courses and Webinars: Learning from Experts

Enrolling in online courses and attending webinars offers a structured way to enhance your investment knowledge. These resources provide a comprehensive learning experience, covering a wide range of topics from the basics of stock market investing to advanced strategies. For example, online courses often include modules on financial markets, investment strategies, and risk management, offering a well-rounded education. Webinars, on the other hand, provide the unique benefit of real-time interaction with industry experts. You can ask questions, clarify doubts, and gain insights that might not be available in written materials. This interactive element makes webinars particularly valuable, as you get to engage with experts and peers, enriching your understanding of complex topics.

When it comes to reputable platforms, Coursera stands out as a top choice for high-quality investment courses. Coursera partners with top universities and institutions to offer courses on various aspects of investing. For example, Yale University's "Financial Markets" course covers the basics of financial markets, while Rice University offers a specialization in "Investment and Portfolio Management." These courses are designed to cater to different skill levels, from beginners to advanced investors. Udemy is another excellent platform that provides a variety of investment courses. Whether you're looking to understand the fundamentals or dive into specific areas like real estate investing or cryptocurrency, Udemy has courses tailored to your needs. The flexibility of these platforms allows you to learn at your own pace, making it easier to fit education into your busy schedule.

Selecting the right courses and webinars is crucial to ensure that your learning aligns with your investment goals. Start by looking for courses with positive reviews and high ratings from past participants. Reviews can provide insights into the course's quality, the instructor's expertise, and the usefulness of the material. Additionally, choose webinars that focus on specific areas of interest. For instance, if you're interested in stock analysis, look for webinars that delve into technical and fundamental analysis. If you're planning for retirement, opt for sessions that cover retirement planning and long-term investment strategies. Many platforms also offer previews or sample lectures, allowing you to gauge whether the course content meets your expectations.

To get the most out of online courses and webinars, actively participate and engage with the material. Take advantage of interactive features such as discussion forums and Q&A sessions. These platforms often have communities where you can discuss topics, ask questions, and share insights with fellow learners. Engaging in these discussions can deepen your understanding and provide different perspectives on the material. Set aside dedicated time to complete course assignments and review materials. Treat your online learning as you would a traditional class, with scheduled study times and a commitment to completing assignments. This disciplined approach ensures that you absorb the material and can apply it effectively in your investment decisions.

7.4 Joining Investment Clubs: The Benefits of Community

Investment clubs offer a collaborative environment where you can pool knowledge, share insights, and make joint investment decisions. These clubs are groups of individuals who come together to discuss investment strategies and goals. Members meet regularly to share research, analyze stocks, and make collective decisions on where to invest their money. This collaborative approach allows you to learn from others, gain new perspectives, and benefit from the group's collective wisdom. Investment clubs can be particularly beneficial for beginners, as they provide a supportive community where you can ask questions, share experiences, and learn from more experienced investors.

Joining an investment club can significantly enhance your investment knowledge and skills. These clubs provide opportunities to learn from others and gain new insights into different investment strategies. Collaborative decision-making can lead to more informed and diversified investment choices. For example, discussing a potential investment with club members can help you identify risks and opportunities that you might have missed on your own. Additionally, investment clubs often have guest speakers and educational sessions where industry experts share their knowledge. These sessions can provide valuable insights and help you stay updated on market trends and investment opportunities.

Finding and joining an investment club is relatively straightforward. You can search for local investment clubs through community centers, libraries, or online directories. Platforms like Meetup and Facebook groups also have communities focused on investing, where you can find and join clubs that align with your interests. When choosing a club, consider the group's focus and goals. Some clubs might focus on specific types of investments, such as stocks, real estate, or cryptocurrencies, while others might have a broader approach. Joining a club that aligns with your investment goals ensures that you gain relevant knowledge and experience.

As a member of an investment club, it's essential to actively participate and contribute to the group's success. Be prepared to share your research and insights during meetings. This collaborative approach ensures that everyone benefits from the collective knowledge and experience of the group. Respect the club's rules and guidelines, and work collaboratively towards common investment goals. This cooperative spirit fosters a supportive and enriching environment where everyone can learn and grow. Additionally, take advantage of the resources and opportunities provided by the club, such as guest speakers, educational sessions, and networking events. These resources can significantly enhance your investment knowledge and skills, helping you become a more informed and confident investor.

7.5 Tracking Your Progress: Tools and Techniques

Regularly monitoring and evaluating your investment performance is crucial for success. Tracking your progress helps you identify areas for improvement and make necessary adjustments to your strategy. For example, suppose you notice that a particular investment isn't performing as expected. In that case, you can analyze the reasons and decide whether to hold, sell, or adjust your position. Regular reviews can increase accountability and ensure you stay on track toward your financial goals. By assessing your portfolio's performance, you can make informed decisions that align with your investment objectives and risk tolerance.

Various tools and platforms can make it easy to monitor your investment performance. Personal finance apps like Mint or YNAB can help you track your investment portfolio alongside your overall finances. These apps provide a comprehensive view of your financial situation, allowing you to see how your investments fit into your broader financial plan. Investment platforms like Morningstar and Yahoo Finance offer portfolio tracking features and performance analysis. These tools provide detailed insights into your investments, including returns, risk metrics, and comparisons to benchmarks. By using these tools, you can stay informed about your portfolio's performance and make data-driven decisions.

Setting up a tracking system is relatively straightforward. Start by listing all your investments and their current values in a spreadsheet or tracking tool. Add columns for essential metrics like purchase price, current price, dividends received, and total returns. Set regular intervals, such as monthly or quarterly, to update and review your portfolio's performance. This regular review process helps you stay on top of your investments and identify any necessary adjustments. For example, if you notice that a particular sector is underperforming, you can decide whether to rebalance your portfolio to reduce exposure to that sector. Regular tracking also helps you stay informed about your progress toward your financial goals, providing motivation and accountability.

Key metrics to monitor include:

- Your portfolio's overall return on investment (ROI)

- Individual asset performance

- Comparison to relevant benchmarks or indices

Monitoring ROI helps you assess the efficiency of your investments and identify areas for improvement. Tracking individual asset performance allows you to see which investments are performing well and which ones might need attention. Comparing your portfolio's performance to benchmarks or indices provides context. It helps you understand how your investments are doing relative to the broader market. By keeping an eye on these metrics, you can make informed decisions and adjust your strategy to optimize your portfolio's performance.

To make your tracking system even more effective, consider setting up alerts and notifications. Many investment platforms and apps allow you to set price alerts, dividend announcements, and other notifications. These alerts keep you informed about significant changes in your investments, allowing you to react promptly. For instance, if one of your stocks suddenly drops in price, an alert can prompt you to investigate the cause and decide on the best course of action.

Similarly, dividend alerts can inform you when dividends are paid, helping you keep track of your income. This proactive approach ensures you stay engaged with your investments, making timely decisions to optimize your portfolio's performance.

By regularly tracking your progress and monitoring key metrics, you stay informed and prepared to make data-driven decisions. This ongoing process helps you refine your investment strategy, ensuring it remains aligned with your financial goals. As you become more comfortable with tracking and analyzing your investments, you'll find it easier to navigate the stock market, making informed decisions that enhance your financial success. Your investment journey becomes more structured and intentional, leading to better outcomes and greater financial confidence.

Incorporating these tracking tools and techniques into your routine not only enhances your investment performance but also builds your financial literacy. The more you engage with your investments, the better you'll understand market dynamics and investment principles. This continuous learning process keeps you ahead of the curve, enabling you to adapt to changing market conditions and seize new opportunities. As you move forward, these habits will become second nature, empowering you to achieve your financial goals and secure your financial future.

Chapter 8
Building Financial Resilience

"A big part of financial freedom is having your heart and mind free from worry about the what-ifs of life."

Suze Orman

I remember a time when the market was in turmoil, and I was filled with anxiety. The headlines were screaming about economic downturns, and my portfolio was taking a hit. I felt a knot in my stomach every time I checked my investments. It was during this period that I learned the true importance of being flexible with my investment strategy. Flexibility became my safety net, allowing me to navigate the stormy waters of market volatility and come out stronger on the other side.

8.1 Adapting to Market Changes: Staying Flexible

The importance of flexibility in investing cannot be overstated. Market conditions can change rapidly due to various factors such as economic events, geopolitical tensions, or technological advancements. For instance, a sudden change in government policy can impact entire industries overnight. Being flexible allows you to adjust your investment strategy to mitigate risks and capitalize on new opportunities as they arise. This adaptability is crucial for maintaining a resilient portfolio in an ever-changing financial landscape.

To stay flexible, one of the most effective strategies is diversification. By spreading your investments across various asset classes and sectors, you reduce your dependency on any single investment. This approach not only mitigates risk but also positions you to benefit from different market conditions. For example, while stocks might be underperforming, your investments in bonds or real estate might be doing well, providing a buffer against losses. Diversification acts as a financial cushion, absorbing the shocks that can come from market volatility.

Another practical tip for maintaining flexibility is to keep a portion of your portfolio in liquid assets. Liquid assets are those that can be easily converted into cash without significant loss of value. Examples include cash, money market funds, and certain types of bonds. Having liquid assets on hand provides you with the agility to respond quickly to market changes. If a sudden investment opportunity arises, you won't be scrambling to free up funds. Likewise, if you need to exit an investment swiftly to avoid losses, liquid assets offer the flexibility to do so without delay.

Ongoing education plays a pivotal role in staying adaptable. The financial world is dynamic, and continuous learning is essential to keep up with market trends and economic indicators. Staying updated on the latest news and developments can help you anticipate potential shifts and make informed decisions. Attend webinars, read financial news, and engage with investment communities to broaden your knowledge. These activities not only keep you informed but also expose you to different perspectives and strategies that can enhance your investment approach.

Consider the case of an investor who successfully adapted to market changes by shifting to defensive stocks during an economic downturn. Defensive stocks are those of companies that provide essential goods and services, such as utilities, healthcare, and consumer staples. These stocks tend to be less sensitive to economic cycles and can provide stability during turbulent times. By reallocating their portfolio to include more defensive stocks, this investor was able to protect their investments and maintain steady returns even when the broader market was struggling.

Another example is an investor who diversified into emerging markets to take advantage of growth opportunities. Emerging markets, such as those in Asia and Latin America, often offer higher growth potential compared to developed markets. However, they also come with higher risks due to factors like political instability and currency fluctuations. By carefully researching and selecting high-potential investments in these regions, this investor was able to capitalize on the rapid economic growth and enhance their portfolio's performance.

Incorporating these strategies into your investment approach can significantly enhance your financial resilience. Flexibility ensures that you are not locked into a rigid plan that might not hold up under changing conditions. It allows you to pivot, adapt, and thrive in the face of uncertainty. Whether it's through diversification, maintaining liquidity, or ongoing education, staying flexible is key to navigating the ever-evolving landscape of investing.

8.2 Emergency Funds: Your Financial Safety Net

Imagine waking up one morning to find your car won't start, and after a trip to the mechanic, you're hit with a hefty repair bill. Or perhaps you receive an unexpected medical bill that isn't fully covered by insurance. These scenarios underscore the importance of an emergency fund—a reserve of money set aside to cover unexpected expenses or financial emergencies. Having an emergency fund can prevent you from having to liquidate your investments at a loss during unforeseen events, providing a crucial buffer that maintains your financial stability.

Building an emergency fund starts with setting a clear savings goal. A good rule of thumb is to save enough to cover three to six months' worth of living expenses. This amount should be tailored to your individual circumstances, considering factors such as job stability, income level, and monthly expenses. For instance, if your monthly expenses total $2,500, aim to save between $7,500 and $15,000. Begin by assessing your current financial situation and determining a realistic monthly savings target. Automate the process by setting up regular transfers to a dedicated emergency fund account, ensuring consistent progress without the need for constant oversight.

Choosing the right place to store your emergency fund is crucial. It should be easily accessible and safe from market volatility. Consider a high-yield savings account, which offers the benefit of earning interest while keeping your funds readily available. Avoid investing your emergency fund in volatile assets like stocks or mutual funds, as their value can fluctuate, potentially leaving you short during a crisis. The goal is not to grow this money aggressively but to ensure it is there when you need it.

The benefits of having an emergency fund extend far beyond just financial security. It can significantly reduce financial stress, providing a sense of security and peace of mind. Knowing that you have a financial cushion allows you to handle unexpected expenses without disrupting your long-term investment strategy. For example, if your water heater breaks down, you can cover the repair costs without having to sell off part of your stock portfolio at a potentially inopportune time. This financial safety net ensures that your investments remain intact and continue to grow, aligned with your long-term goals.

Interactive Element: Emergency Fund Checklist

1. **Set a Savings Goal:** Calculate three to six months' worth of living expenses.

2. **Automate Savings:** Set up regular transfers to a dedicated emergency fund account.

3. **Choose the Right Account:** Opt for a high-yield savings account for accessibility and interest.

4. **Monitor Progress:** Regularly check your balance and adjust contributions as needed.

5. **Use Wisely:** Only tap into this fund for true emergencies to ensure it

remains available when needed.

Following these steps can help you build and maintain a robust emergency fund, providing a crucial layer of protection against financial shocks. This fund is not just a financial tool but a cornerstone of a resilient financial plan, enabling you to weather life's uncertainties with confidence and stability.

8.3 The Role of Insurance in Financial Planning

Insurance is a critical component of financial planning, acting as a safety net that protects against unexpected financial risks. Imagine facing significant medical bills after an accident or dealing with property damage from a natural disaster. Without insurance, these events can lead to significant financial setbacks, draining your savings and jeopardizing your financial stability. Insurance helps cover these substantial expenses, allowing you to maintain your financial health and protect your assets and investments from unforeseen events. For instance, health insurance can cover medical costs, preventing high out-of-pocket expenses that could otherwise deplete your emergency fund or savings.

There are various types of insurance, each serving a unique purpose in safeguarding different aspects of your life. Health insurance, for example, covers medical expenses, including doctor visits, hospital stays, and prescription medications. This type of insurance is crucial for managing healthcare costs and ensuring you receive necessary medical care without financial strain. Life insurance, on the other hand, provides financial support to your dependents in the event of your death. It ensures that your loved ones are financially secure and can cover expenses such as mortgage payments, education costs, and daily living expenses. Disability insurance is another vital coverage, replacing a portion of your income if you become unable to work due to illness or injury. This coverage helps maintain your financial stability and supports your living expenses during recovery.

Selecting the right insurance policies requires careful consideration of your personal and financial situation. Assess your needs based on factors such as your age, health, income, and family responsibilities. For instance, young professionals might prioritize health and disability insurance, while those with dependents should consider life insurance. Compare policies from different providers to find the best coverage at an affordable price. Look for policies that offer comprehensive coverage without excessive premiums. Evaluate the terms and conditions, including coverage limits, exclusions, and deductibles, to ensure the policy aligns with your needs. Consulting with an insurance advisor can also provide valuable insights and help you make informed decisions.

Incorporating insurance into your overall financial strategy involves regular review and adjustment of your coverage. Your insurance needs may change over time due to life events such as marriage, childbirth, or career changes. For instance, as you accumulate more assets or take on additional responsibilities, you might need to increase your coverage limits or add new policies. Regularly reviewing your insurance ensures that your coverage remains adequate and relevant to your current financial goals and circumstances. Working with a financial advisor can help integrate insurance planning with your investment and retirement strategies. This holistic approach ensures that all aspects of your financial plan work together to provide comprehensive protection and support your long-term objectives.

Consider the case of a young couple who recently purchased their first home and welcomed their first child. They realized the importance of protecting their growing family and financial investments. They assessed their needs and decided to purchase life insurance to ensure their child's future is secure, even in the event of an untimely death. They also opted for disability insurance to safeguard against the loss of income due to illness or injury. By integrating these insurance policies into their financial plan, they created a robust safety net that provides peace of mind and financial security. Regular reviews of their policies ensure that their coverage evolves with their changing needs, such as when they plan for more children or consider higher education expenses.

Another example involves a professional who experienced a severe health issue that temporarily affected their ability to work. Thanks to their disability insurance, they received a portion of their income during the recovery period, allowing them to focus on rehabilitation without worrying about financial instability. This experience highlighted the importance of having the right insurance coverage. It prompted them to regularly review and adjust their policies to address new risks and life changes.

Incorporating insurance into your financial plan is not just about protecting against risks—it's about creating a resilient financial foundation that supports your goals and aspirations. By understanding the role of different types of insurance, selecting appropriate coverage, and integrating it into your comprehensive financial strategy, you can safeguard your financial well-being and ensure that you are prepared for whatever life throws your way.

8.4 Handling Financial Setbacks: Recovering and Moving Forward

Life is full of surprises, and not all of them are pleasant. Financial setbacks such as job loss, medical emergencies, or unexpected expenses can throw a wrench into even the most well-laid plans. Imagine losing your job unexpectedly. The sudden decrease in income can be jarring, requiring immediate adjustments to your budget and spending habits. Similarly, a medical emergency, even with health insurance, can result in significant out-of-pocket expenses, straining your finances. These setbacks are not just numbers on a spreadsheet; they are real-life challenges that can affect your peace of mind and financial stability.

When faced with a financial setback, the first step is to assess the situation and create a revised budget. Prioritize essential expenses such as housing, utilities, and groceries. Non-essential expenses, like dining out and entertainment, should be minimized or temporarily eliminated. This reallocation ensures that your basic needs are met while you navigate through the crisis. Additionally, exploring additional income sources can provide a financial cushion. Part-time work, freelancing, or gig economy jobs can supplement your income and help bridge the gap until you regain financial stability. For instance, taking on freelance projects or driving for a ride-sharing service can provide immediate cash flow, easing some of the financial pressure.

Maintaining a positive mindset during financial setbacks is crucial. It's easy to feel overwhelmed and discouraged, but resilience and a proactive attitude can make a significant difference. Stay focused on your long-term goals and avoid making impulsive decisions out of fear or frustration. Lean on your support network—friends, family, or financial advisors can offer valuable advice and emotional support. They can help you see the bigger picture and remind you that setbacks are temporary hurdles, not permanent roadblocks. Keeping a journal to track your progress and reflect on your journey can also provide motivation and a sense of control.

Consider the story of someone who faced job loss but turned the setback into an opportunity for growth. After losing their job, they decided to retrain for a new career, enrolling in online courses to gain new skills. This proactive approach not only helped them secure a new job but also led to a higher-paying position than before. By focusing on personal development and leveraging available resources, they were able to rebuild their savings and achieve greater financial stability. This example underscores the importance of viewing setbacks as opportunities for growth and transformation.

Another inspiring case involves an individual who managed medical debt through strategic planning. Faced with mounting medical bills, they adopted a meticulous budgeting approach, cutting unnecessary expenses and prioritizing debt repayment. They also negotiated with healthcare providers for more manageable payment plans and sought financial assistance from charitable organizations. Through disciplined budgeting and resourcefulness, they gradually paid off their medical debt and restored their financial health. This experience highlights the power of persistence, strategic planning, and seeking help when needed.

Navigating financial setbacks requires a combination of practical strategies and a resilient mindset. By assessing the situation, adjusting your budget, exploring additional income sources, and maintaining a positive attitude, you can recover and move forward with confidence. Remember, setbacks are part of life's financial landscape, but with the right approach, they can be managed and even turned into opportunities for growth and improvement.

8.5 Cultivating a Positive Money Mindset: Financial Wellness

A money mindset refers to your attitudes and beliefs about money. It's the lens through which you view your finances and make decisions. A positive money mindset can significantly impact how you manage and grow your finances. It encourages you to see opportunities rather than obstacles, helping you make informed decisions, stay motivated, and achieve your financial goals. For example, if you believe that money is a tool for freedom and security, you're more likely to take proactive steps to save, invest, and plan for the future.

Cultivating a positive money mindset offers numerous benefits. It can reduce financial stress by increasing your confidence in managing money effectively. When you view money positively, you're more likely to engage in proactive financial planning, which fosters a sense of control over your financial future. This mindset encourages you to set clear goals, make informed decisions, and stay committed to your financial plan. It helps you navigate financial challenges with resilience and optimism, knowing that you have the tools and knowledge to overcome them.

Developing a positive money mindset involves several practical strategies. First, set clear financial goals and celebrate small milestones to stay motivated and focused. Achieving these milestones provides a sense of accomplishment and reinforces positive financial behaviors. For example, if your goal is to save $1,000, celebrate when you reach $100, $500, and so on. These celebrations can be simple, like treating yourself to a nice meal or enjoying a day out.

Practicing gratitude is another powerful strategy. Recognize and appreciate the progress you've made in your financial journey. This practice shifts your focus from what you lack to what you have achieved, fostering a more positive outlook. For instance, take a few minutes each day to reflect on financial successes, no matter how small. Whether it's paying off a credit card, sticking to your budget for a month, or investing in your first stock, acknowledging these achievements can boost your morale and encourage continued progress.

Educating yourself about personal finance is crucial for building confidence and reducing anxiety. The more you understand money management, the more empowered you feel to make intelligent financial decisions. Read books, attend workshops, and follow financial news to stay informed. For example, reading a book like "Rich Dad Poor Dad" can provide valuable insights into building wealth and making money work for you. Engaging with financial content regularly helps reinforce positive financial habits and keeps you motivated to continue learning and growing.

Consider the story of someone who overcame debt by changing their spending habits and focusing on long-term goals. Initially, they struggled with credit card debt and felt overwhelmed. However, by adopting a positive money mindset, they began to see debt as a challenge to overcome rather than a permanent burden. They created a budget, cut unnecessary expenses, and committed to paying off their debt. Each month, they celebrated small victories, like reducing their debt by a specific amount. Over time, they eliminated their debt, built an emergency fund, and started investing for the future. This transformation was driven by a shift in mindset from defeat to determination.

Another example involves an individual who built wealth by adopting a growth mindset and continuously learning about investing. Initially, they knew little about the stock market and felt intimidated by the complexity of investing. However, they decided to educate themselves by reading books, attending seminars, and seeking advice from experienced investors. This commitment to learning helped them develop a positive attitude towards investing. They started with small investments, gradually increasing their portfolio as their confidence grew. Over the years, their investments flourished, and they achieved financial independence. This success story highlights the power of a growth mindset in driving financial success.

Cultivating a positive money mindset is not just about improving your financial situation; it's about enhancing your overall well-being. A healthy attitude towards money can lead to a more fulfilling and balanced life. By setting clear goals, practicing gratitude, and continuously educating yourself, you can develop a mindset that supports financial wellness and empowers you to achieve your dreams.

Remember, your mindset shapes your financial reality. By adopting a positive and proactive approach to money, you can navigate financial challenges with confidence and build a secure, prosperous future. This chapter has explored the importance of flexibility, the necessity of emergency funds, the role of insurance, and how to handle financial setbacks. Each of these elements contributes to building financial resilience and preparing you for life's uncertainties.

Chapter 9

Empowerment and Independence

"No one can make you feel inferior without your consent."
Eleanor Roosevelt

I remember a time when I felt completely lost in my financial life. I had student loans piling up, credit card debt, and no clear path forward. One day, while browsing in a bookstore, I stumbled upon a book about personal finance. It was as if a light bulb went off in my head. That moment marked the beginning of my journey toward financial empowerment. I devoured the book, followed its advice, and slowly but surely, I began to take control of my financial destiny. This chapter aims to provide you with the tools and strategies to do the same.

9.1 Taking Control of Your Financial Destiny: Empowerment Strategies

Financial empowerment is more than just having money in the bank; it's about making informed decisions and taking proactive steps toward your financial goals. When you are financially empowered, you can navigate the complexities of the financial world with confidence. This empowerment fosters a sense of control over your financial future, allowing you to make decisions that align with your long-term goals. For example, financial empowerment enables you to evaluate investment opportunities critically, ensuring that your choices are well-informed and strategically sound. This level of control can significantly reduce financial stress, providing peace of mind and a more straightforward path to achieving your financial objectives.

One of the first steps toward financial empowerment is creating a detailed financial plan. This plan should outline your financial goals, strategies, and timelines. Start by identifying both short-term and long-term goals. Short-term goals might include building an emergency fund or paying off credit card debt, while long-term goals could involve saving for a down payment on a house or planning for retirement. Once your goals are clear, develop strategies to achieve them. This might include setting up automatic transfers to a savings account, investing in a diversified portfolio, or cutting unnecessary expenses. Regularly review and adjust your plan to stay on track and accommodate changes in your life. Life is dynamic, and your financial plan should be flexible enough to adapt to new circumstances, such as a change in income, unexpected expenses, or shifts in your financial goals.

Continuous learning is another crucial aspect of financial empowerment. The financial landscape is ever-evolving, and staying informed is critical to making sound financial decisions. Invest in your financial education by reading books, taking courses, and attending seminars. For instance, books like "The Intelligent Investor" by Benjamin Graham can provide valuable insights into investment strategies, while online courses can offer structured learning on various financial topics. Additionally, staying updated on market trends and economic developments can help you make informed decisions. Subscribe to financial newsletters, follow reputable financial news sources, and participate in investment forums. This ongoing education will not only enhance your financial literacy but also keep you abreast of new opportunities and potential risks in the financial world.

Consider the story of Jane, a young professional who faced significant financial challenges early in her career. Jane had accumulated substantial student debt and was struggling to manage her finances. Determined to take control of her financial destiny, she created a comprehensive financial plan that included a detailed budget, a debt repayment strategy, and an investment plan. Jane also invested time in educating herself about personal finance, reading books, attending workshops, and seeking advice from financial experts. Over time, her disciplined approach paid off. She successfully paid off her student loans, built a robust emergency fund, and started investing for her future. Jane's story is a testament to the power of financial empowerment and the positive impact it can have on one's life.

By taking control of your financial destiny, you can achieve a sense of independence and security. This control enables you to make informed decisions, take proactive steps toward your goals, and navigate the financial landscape with confidence. Remember, financial empowerment is a journey, and every step you take brings you closer to achieving your financial dreams.

9.2 Aligning Investments with Personal Values: Ethical Choices

Value-based investing is about more than just growing your wealth; it's about aligning your money with your principles. This approach lets you invest in companies and industries that reflect your ethical beliefs, creating a portfolio that supports causes you care about. For instance, if environmental sustainability is important to you, you might choose to invest in companies that prioritize green technologies and have a low carbon footprint. This way, your investments not only aim for financial returns but also contribute to positive societal and environmental impacts.

One of the significant benefits of ethical investing is the sense of fulfillment it brings. Knowing that your money is backing companies with responsible practices can provide a deeper sense of purpose. It's gratifying to realize that your investments are not just about personal gain but also about supporting positive changes in the world. Moreover, companies with strong ethical practices often exhibit better long-term performance and stability. Businesses that prioritize environmental, social, and governance (ESG) factors tend to be more resilient and better positioned to adapt to changing regulations and market conditions.

To select ethical investments, look for companies with transparent ESG reporting. This transparency indicates a company's commitment to responsible practices. It helps you assess its performance in areas like environmental impact, social responsibility, and corporate governance. Funds and ETFs focusing on ethical and sustainable investments can also be a good option. These financial products aggregate investments in companies that meet specific ESG criteria, offering diversification while aligning with your values. For example, an ESG-focused ETF might include companies with robust environmental policies, fair labor practices, and transparent governance structures.

Ethical investing can significantly impact society by encouraging companies to adopt more responsible practices. When investors collectively prioritize ESG factors, they can pressure companies to improve their environmental and social policies. Investing in green technologies, for instance, supports environmental sustainability and reduces carbon footprints. Similarly, supporting companies with fair labor practices promotes social justice and improves working conditions. This shift not only benefits society but also creates a more stable and sustainable market environment.

Consider the impact of your investments on broader societal goals. For example, choosing to invest in renewable energy companies supports the transition to a more sustainable energy system. Similarly, investing in companies with substantial diversity and inclusion policies can promote social equity and innovation. Value-based investing allows you to use your financial power to support the changes you want to see in the world. By aligning your investments with your personal values, you can contribute to a positive future while working toward your financial goals.

9.3 Achieving Financial Independence: Long-Term Strategies

Financial independence means having enough wealth to cover your living expenses without needing to rely on employment income. Imagine waking up each day with the freedom to pursue your passions, whether it's traveling, starting a new hobby, or spending time with loved ones, all without financial constraints.

Achieving this state requires a strategic approach focused on building and managing wealth effectively.

To reach financial independence, start by maximizing your savings and investments. It begins with disciplined budgeting and spending. Track your expenses meticulously and identify areas where you can cut back. Redirect these savings into investments that offer growth potential. Diversification is critical here; by spreading your investments across different asset classes, you reduce risk and increase the chances of stable returns. Consider a mix of stocks, bonds, and real estate to create a balanced portfolio. Regularly review your investments to ensure they align with your financial goals and adjust as necessary.

Creating multiple income streams can significantly accelerate your path to financial independence. Diversifying your sources of income reduces reliance on a single paycheck and provides financial stability. Look into side hustles or freelance work that leverages your skills and interests. For instance, if you enjoy writing, consider freelance writing gigs. Passive income sources like rental properties or dividend stocks can also contribute to your income without requiring active effort. Exploring entrepreneurship is another powerful avenue. Starting your own business, even as a small side project, can grow into a substantial income source over time. The key is to identify opportunities that align with your skills and passions, ensuring sustainable and enjoyable income streams.

Consider the story of Mark, who achieved financial independence by investing in real estate. Mark started with a single rental property, diligently saving and reinvesting the rental income. Over the years, he expanded his portfolio to include multiple properties, generating a steady stream of passive income. His disciplined approach and strategic planning allowed him to retire early and focus on his passion for travel. Another example is Emily, who combined a high savings rate with smart investing. She consistently saved a significant portion of her income and invested in low-cost index funds. By living below her means and making informed investment choices, Emily reached financial independence in her forties, giving her the freedom to pursue her dream of writing a novel.

These success stories highlight the importance of strategic planning and disciplined execution in achieving financial independence. By maximizing savings, diversifying investments, and creating multiple income streams, you can build the financial foundation needed to live life on your terms.

9.4 The Importance of Mentorship: Learning from Others

Mentorship can be a game-changer in your financial growth. Learning from someone who has already navigated the complexities of investing and personal finance can save you time and help you avoid common mistakes. Mentors offer valuable insights, sharing their successes and failures, which can provide you with a more straightforward path. Imagine having a seasoned investor guide you through your first major investment decision, offering advice based on years of experience. This guidance can be invaluable, helping you make informed choices and navigate complex financial situations with greater ease.

Finding the right mentor starts with identifying individuals who have achieved success in areas relevant to your financial goals. Look for someone with a proven track record in investing, financial planning, or any other area you're interested in. Industry professionals, networking groups, and mentorship programs are excellent places to start. For example, joining a local investment club or attending financial seminars can expose you to potential mentors. When reaching out, be specific about how their guidance could benefit you and what you hope to achieve through the mentorship. This clarity shows that you value their time and expertise, making it more likely they will be willing to help you.

A successful mentor-mentee relationship is built on mutual respect and reciprocity. Show appreciation for your mentor's time and insights by being respectful and committed. This means showing up prepared for meetings, asking thoughtful questions, and actively implementing their advice. Look for opportunities to provide value to your mentor as well. It could be as simple as sharing your own knowledge, offering assistance on a project, or providing feedback on their work. This reciprocal relationship not only strengthens the bond but also ensures that both parties benefit from the mentoring experience.

Consider the story of David, an aspiring entrepreneur who found a mentor in a successful startup founder. With his mentor's guidance, David navigated the challenges of scaling his business, from securing funding to managing a growing team. His mentor's advice helped him avoid pitfalls and make strategic decisions that led to substantial business growth. Another example is Lisa, who achieved investment success through the mentorship of an experienced financial advisor. Her mentor guided her through market analysis, portfolio diversification, and risk management, enabling her to build a robust investment portfolio. These examples highlight how mentorship can accelerate financial success by providing practical advice and support.

9.5 Giving Back: The Role of Philanthropy

Philanthropy is about more than just writing checks; it's about creating meaningful change in the world. By donating time, money, or resources to support charitable causes, you contribute to society's welfare and make a positive impact. This act of giving back not only helps those in need but also brings a sense of fulfillment and purpose to your life. Knowing that your contributions are making a difference can provide immense personal satisfaction. Whether you're funding educational programs, supporting healthcare initiatives, or volunteering at local shelters, philanthropy allows you to play an active role in improving the well-being of others.

The benefits of giving back extend beyond personal fulfillment. Engaging in philanthropic activities can also enhance your financial well-being. By supporting causes that resonate with your values, you build a positive legacy and inspire others to contribute to meaningful causes. This ripple effect can lead to a more compassionate and supportive community, fostering a culture of giving. Philanthropy can also provide tax benefits, as many charitable donations are tax-deductible. This financial incentive can make your contributions even more impactful, allowing you to support the causes you care about while also benefiting from reduced tax liabilities.

To engage in effective philanthropy, it's crucial to choose charitable causes and organizations that align with your values and interests. Start by identifying issues that resonate with you, whether it's environmental conservation, education, or social justice. Research organizations to ensure they are reputable and use donations effectively. Look for transparent reporting on how funds are allocated and the impact they achieve. Websites like Charity Navigator and GuideStar can provide valuable insights into the credibility and efficiency of various nonprofits. By supporting organizations that align with your values and demonstrate effective use of resources, you can maximize the impact of your philanthropic efforts.

Consider the story of Alex, who established a charitable foundation to support education and healthcare initiatives in underserved communities. Through his foundation, Alex has funded scholarships for students, built schools, and supported healthcare clinics. His philanthropic efforts have not only improved the lives of countless individuals but also brought him a deep sense of purpose and fulfillment. Another example is Maria, an investor who donates a portion of her investment gains to environmental conservation projects. By supporting initiatives that protect natural habitats and promote sustainability, Maria has made a significant impact on the environment while also aligning her financial success with her values.

These stories illustrate how integrating philanthropy into your financial life can create positive change and bring personal satisfaction. By giving back, you contribute to the betterment of society while also enriching your own life. Whether through financial donations, volunteering, or establishing charitable foundations, your efforts can make a lasting impact. Philanthropy is an opportunity to use your resources to support the causes you care about, leaving a meaningful legacy for future generations.

9.6 Celebrating Milestones: Recognizing Your Progress

Celebrating financial milestones is more than just a pat on the back; it's a vital part of staying motivated on your path to financial success. When you acknowledge achievements, you recognize the progress you've made and maintain momentum toward your long-term goals. Imagine the satisfaction of reaching your first savings target or paying off a significant chunk of debt. These moments are worth celebrating because they mark your dedication and hard work. Celebrating provides an opportunity to reflect on your achievements, appreciate the steps you've taken, and recharge for the journey ahead. This recognition is crucial for keeping your spirits high and your motivation strong.

Setting meaningful milestones is the first step in making your financial journey rewarding. Start by defining specific, measurable milestones that align with your financial goals. For instance, you might set a goal to save a certain amount each month, reach a net worth target, or pay off a particular debt. These milestones should be clear and attainable, providing a roadmap for your financial journey. Once you've set these milestones, think about how you will celebrate them. Celebrations should be personal and meaningful to you. Whether it's treating yourself to a special experience, sharing your success with loved ones, or taking a day off to relax and reflect, make sure the celebration feels rewarding. This positive reinforcement encourages continued effort and commitment to your financial plan, building confidence and reinforcing the belief that you can achieve your goals.

Positive reinforcement is a powerful tool in maintaining financial discipline. Celebrating milestones helps solidify positive financial behaviors and habits. When you reward yourself for reaching a goal, you create a positive association with the actions that led to that achievement. This reinforcement makes it more likely that you will continue to practice these good habits. For example, if you celebrate reaching a savings target by treating yourself to a nice dinner, you'll associate the discipline of saving with positive outcomes. This approach builds a cycle of motivation and reward, making it easier to stick to your financial plan over the long term.

Consider Sarah, who celebrated paying off her student loans by taking a dream vacation. This celebration marked the end of a long journey and the beginning of a new chapter in her financial life. It was a way to acknowledge her hard work and dedication, providing a well-deserved break and a fresh start. Another example is the Johnson family, who marked reaching their savings goal by hosting a celebratory dinner. They invited close friends and family to share in their achievements, making the moment even more special. These celebrations not only recognized their accomplishments but also provided motivation to continue working toward their next financial goals.

Celebrating financial milestones is an integral part of maintaining motivation and momentum on your path to financial independence. By setting meaningful milestones, celebrating achievements in personal ways, and using positive reinforcement, you can stay motivated and committed to your financial goals. Recognizing your progress helps you appreciate the journey, build confidence, and reinforce the belief that you can achieve your financial dreams.

9.7 Sharing Your Knowledge: Helping Others Start Their Journey

Sharing financial knowledge can create a ripple effect, empowering others to take control of their financial future and achieve their goals. When you share what you've learned, you contribute to building a financially literate and resilient community. Imagine the impact of helping a friend understand how to budget effectively; you're not just aiding them in managing their money better, but also fostering a culture of financial awareness.

To effectively share financial knowledge, start with your own experiences and the lessons you've learned along the way. Use clear and simple language to explain financial concepts, avoiding jargon that might confuse beginners. If you managed to get out of debt, talk about the strategies you used. If you started investing with a small amount, share how you did it and the results. Personal stories make the information relatable and easier to understand.

Mentoring others in personal finance can also offer significant personal growth and fulfillment. When you teach someone else, you reinforce your own knowledge and sharpen your financial skills. It creates a sense of purpose and satisfaction, knowing you are making a positive difference in someone else's life. For instance, guiding a friend through their first investment can deepen your own understanding of the market and solidify your strategies.

Consider the story of Rachel, who helped her cousin create a budget and start investing. Rachel shared her budgeting templates and investment strategies, guiding her cousin every step of the way. Her cousin not only gained financial stability but also started to invest confidently. Another example is Danny, a community leader who organized financial literacy workshops for local residents. He covered topics like saving, investing, and debt management, equipping attendees with the knowledge to improve their financial situations.

These examples highlight the profound impact of sharing financial knowledge. By mentoring others, you help them build the skills needed to achieve their financial goals, while also enriching your own understanding and sense of purpose. Imagine the satisfaction of seeing someone you mentored succeed, knowing that you played a part in their journey toward financial independence. Your efforts can create a ripple effect, fostering a community where financial literacy and resilience are the norms.

9.8 Your Financial Future: Next Steps and Beyond

Planning for the future is not a one-time task but an ongoing process. It's about setting new goals, adapting to changes, and continuously improving your financial strategy. Life is full of uncertainties and opportunities, and having a robust plan ensures you're prepared for both. Regularly reviewing and updating your financial goals is crucial. As your life evolves, so too will your financial needs and aspirations. Whether it's planning for retirement, estate planning, or legacy building, staying adaptable allows you to navigate life's twists and turns with confidence and clarity.

To set future financial goals, start by identifying what truly matters to you. Break these goals down into manageable steps. For example, if your long-term goal is to retire comfortably, consider what steps are needed to achieve that. It might include maximizing contributions to retirement accounts, diversifying your investment portfolio, and regularly assessing your progress. Prioritize these goals based on your current life stage and financial situation. It's also essential to remain flexible, as priorities can shift over time. Regularly reviewing your goals helps keep them aligned with your evolving aspirations and circumstances.

Continuous learning and improvement play a pivotal role in achieving long-term financial success. The financial landscape is ever-changing, with new market trends, economic developments, and investment opportunities emerging regularly. Staying informed is vital. Invest in your financial education through books, courses, and professional advice. For instance, attending seminars or enrolling in online courses can provide valuable insights into advanced investment strategies. Keeping up with financial news and trends helps you make informed decisions and seize new opportunities. This commitment to ongoing learning ensures that your financial knowledge and skills remain sharp and relevant.

Consider the story of Tom, who built a diversified investment portfolio that enabled him to retire early. Tom started investing in his twenties, focusing on a mix of stocks, bonds, and real estate. He regularly reviewed his portfolio and adjusted his strategy based on market conditions and his financial goals. This disciplined approach allowed him to achieve financial independence by his late forties. Another example is Laura, who created a comprehensive estate plan to ensure her wealth was preserved and passed on to future generations. Laura worked with a financial advisor to establish trusts, draft a will, and set up charitable donations. Her meticulous planning provided peace of mind and secured her family's future.

In summary, planning for the future involves setting and regularly revisiting financial goals, staying adaptable, and continuously enhancing your financial knowledge. These steps ensure you remain prepared for whatever life throws your way. As you continue your financial journey, remember that the goal is not just to accumulate wealth but to build a secure and fulfilling future.

Conclusion

As we come to the end of this guide, let's recap the journey we've taken together. We've explored the fundamentals of stock market investing, starting with the foundational knowledge of stocks, the mechanics of the stock market, and setting up your first brokerage account. We then moved on to practical steps for getting started: selecting your first stocks, budgeting for investments, and making your first trade. We've also delved into the importance of risk management and diversification, understanding financial statements, and making informed decisions based on key indicators and market trends.

Throughout the book, we've emphasized the power of long-term investment strategies, the magic of compounding, and the significance of planning for retirement. We explored dividend stocks for passive income and discussed setting realistic investment goals. We've also covered the importance of staying informed, continuous learning, and joining investment communities for shared knowledge and support.

The key takeaways from this book are simple yet powerful. Start small, but start now. Understand that investing is a journey, not a sprint. Diversification is your friend and risk management is crucial. Stay informed and continuously educate yourself. Set realistic goals and celebrate your milestones. Remember, financial independence is achievable with discipline, patience, and a long-term perspective.

Now, it's time for you to take actionable steps toward your financial goals. Open that brokerage account if you haven't already done so. Start with a modest investment, perhaps as little as $100, and grow from there. Research and select your first stocks or ETFs. Make a plan and stick to it. Regularly review your investments and adjust as needed. And most importantly, don't be afraid to seek help when you need it. Join investment clubs, attend webinars, and engage in online communities.

I want to inspire confidence and motivation in you. Remember, every expert was once a beginner. The stock market may seem daunting, but with the knowledge and tools you've gained, you are well-equipped to navigate it. Take control of your financial destiny. Embrace the ups and downs as part of the learning process. Stay resilient and keep your eyes on your long-term goals. Financial independence is within your reach, and every small step you take brings you closer to it.

I am deeply grateful for the opportunity to share this journey with you. Your commitment to learning and growing is commendable. Know that you are not alone. There is a community of like-minded individuals who are on the same path, and there are countless resources available to support you. Keep learning, keep investing, and keep pushing forward.

Thank you for allowing me to be a part of your financial journey. I wish you all the success and fulfillment in your investing endeavors.

Remember, the road to wealth is not just about financial gain; it's about empowerment, independence, and the freedom to live life on your terms. You've got this!

About The Author

Megan Reed is an experienced investor and the author. Her work delves into investing, aiming to make it accessible to people of all levels and demystify what is often viewed as a complex process.

Megan has been investing for over 20 years and is determined to use her experience in the stock market to help beginner investors gain a strong foothold as they start their investment journeys. She has acquired an in-depth understanding of the market over the years and is passionate about sharing her insights with others.

Megan worked in the public sector for many years and has struggled through turbulent times throughout her working life. Getting started in investment allowed her to avoid financial disaster, which could have left her bankrupt. This was the catalyst for her drive to share her experience with others, particularly women, who are often neglected in investment literature. As her own investment success grew, she escaped the rat race, and she hopes to give other women the tools and information they need to do the same.

Megan is an immigrant to the US and has lived in the States since childhood. She is a regular church-goer and loves spending time with her dog.

Also By Megan Reed

The Ultimate Stock Investing For Beginners Playbook: Discover The 7 Effective Strategies For Women To Obtain Explosive Growth, Escape The Rat Race, And Retire Early

Want a FREE copy of this book? Send a screenshot of your review for the book you just read to my assistant, Paul, at ciscopaul@gmail.com and he will send it to you right away! Thank you for your support.

References

The NYSE and Nasdaq: How They Work https://www.investopedia.com/articles/basics/03/103103.asp

Preferred vs. Common Stock: What's the difference? https://fortune.com/recommends/investing/preferred-stock-vs-common-stock/

Millennials and Financial Literacy: A Global Perspective https://gflec.org/wp-content/uploads/2017/07/Millennials-and-Financial-Literacy-Research-Paper.pdf

How to Open a Brokerage Account: A Step-by-Step Guide https://www.fool.com/the-ascent/buying-stocks/how-to-open-brokerage-account/

Best Online Brokers And Trading Platforms Of September ... https://www.forbes.com/advisor/investing/best-online-brokers/

How to Buy Fractional Shares https://www.investopedia.com/how-to-buy-fractional-shares-7482606

The Importance of Diversification https://www.investopedia.com/investing/importance-diversification/

Best Investment Apps of September 2024 https://millennialmoney.com/best-investment-apps/

Types of investment risk https://www.getsmarteraboutmoney.ca/learning-path/understanding-risk/types-of-investment-risk/

The Importance of Diversification - Investopedia https://www.investopedia.com/investing/importance-diversification/#:~:text=By%20spreading%20your%20investments%20across,increasing%20your%20risk%2Dadjusted%20returns.

The Art of Building a Balanced Portfolio https://www.citizensbank.com/learning/how-to-build-a-balanced-portfolio.aspx

Basics of ETFs for Beginners https://www.ally.com/stories/invest/etfs-for-beginners/

How to Read Financial Statements: A Beginner's Guide https://online.hbs.edu/blog/post/how-to-read-financial-statements

Financial Ratio Analysis: Definition, Types, Examples, and … https://www.investopedia.com/terms/r/ratioanalysis.asp

Understanding Trend Analysis and Trend Trading Strategies https://www.investopedia.com/terms/t/trendanalysis.asp

Best Time(s) of Day, Week, and Month to Trade Stocks https://www.investopedia.com/day-trading/best-time-day-week-month-trade-stocks/

Power of Long-Term Compound Interest Investments https://www.schwab.com/learn/story/power-long-term-compound-interest-investments

Retirement planning for millennials: How to get started and … https://www.principal.com/individuals/build-your-knowledge/retirement-planning-millennials-how-get-started-and-make-progress

Why Dividends Matter - Fidelity https://www.fidelity.com/learning-center/investment-products/stocks/why-dividends-matter

Ethical and ESG fund investing: your complete guide https://www.unbiased.co.uk/discover/personal-finance/savings-investing/ethical-investing

The Influence of Investor Emotion on the Stock Market … https://onlinelibrary.wiley.com/doi/10.1155/2021/5520276

Why overconfidence bias may cost investors https://www.cnbc.com/2023/01/19/why-overconfidence-bias-may-cost-investors.html

The Dangers of Herd Behavior in Investment Decisions https://www.linkedin.com/pulse/dangers-herd-behavior-investment-decisions-christina-chua-mba-

What Is a Brokerage Fee? How Fees Work and Types https://www.investopedia.com/terms/b/brokerage-fee.asp

Bloomberg - Business News, Stock Markets, Finance ... https://www.bloomberg.com/

Top 10 Investment Books for Beginners in 2024 https://finmasters.com/best-investment-books-for-beginners/

Best Investment Courses Online with Certificates [2024] https://www.coursera.org/courses?query=investment

Investment Clubs: How To Join One Or Start Your Own https://www.bankrate.com/investing/how-to-start-join-investment-club/

What Is Investment Flexibility, And Why Is It Important? - Forbes https://www.forbes.com/councils/forbesfinancecouncil/2023/04/10/what-is-investment-flexibility-and-why-is-it-important/#:~:text=Flexibility%20allows%20you%20to%20make,if%20there%20were%20unforeseen%20circumstances.

An essential guide to building an emergency fund https://www.consumerfinance.gov/an-essential-guide-to-building-an-emergency-fund/

5 Types of Insurance to Protect Your Income, Wealth and ... https://www.letsmakeaplan.org/financial-topics/articles/insurance-planning/5-types-of-insurance-to-protect-your-income-wealth-and-family

From Financial Ruin to Recovery: Inspiring Stories of ... https://www.linkedin.com/pulse/from-financial-ruin-recovery-inspiring-stories-survivors-joe-wrobel

Financial planning tips for millennials https://www.rbcwealthmanagement.com/en-ca/insights/financial-planning-tips-for-millennials

Values-Based Investing: How to Align Your Money and ... https://financebuzz.com/values-based-investing

Achieving Financial Independence: A Step-by-Step Guide https://www.playingwithfire.co/blog/how-to-reach-financial-independence

The Importance Of Mentorship https://www.forbes.com/councils/forbesbusinesscouncil/2023/07/05/the-importance-of-mentorship/

www.ingramcontent.com/pod-product-compliance
Lightning Source LLC
Chambersburg PA
CBHW050315230526
45471CB00005B/2187